Ten Thousand Horses

"Stahl-Wert and Jennings have captured, through this poignant story, what it takes to enable high employee engagement that produces sustainable high performance. I heartily recommend this newest work for those who seek to enable uncommon engagement to produce extraordinary results."

P. Douglas Wilson, Vice President, Global Merger

Integration, Boston Scientific Corporation

"*Ten Thousand Horses* is an inspiring story of a business manager facing failure both at work and at home. Managers from either the private or public sector will find *Ten Thousand Horses* helpful in improving their leadership capabilities and in transforming their organizations."

William Sterling, CEO and Chief Investment Officer,

Trilogy Global Advisors

"In this time of great economic change, every business must outperform its competition and execute as flawlessly as possible. *Ten Thousand Horses* forcefully addresses that task head-on and should be read by every leader who wants to make a great impact in their work. Stahl-Wert and Jennings have again brought us a powerful business book and a moving story that will benefit those who use it to improve their operations."

B. Joseph Pine II, coauthor of The Experience Economy

"*Ten Thousand Horses* is a wonderful palimpsest—a three-tiered set of Russian nested dolls. It is a story about strong, beautiful-but-discarded horses inside a story about strong, beautiful-but-discarded teens inside a story about how underperforming work groups get slingshotted to success by strong leaders. The rules for success are easy to understand and allow readers to internalize the 'how' and not just the 'what' of leadership."

Harry Howell, retired CEO, Boston Financial

"*Ten Thousand Horses* grabbed my attention, enlarged my vision, and filled me with a deeper desire to make a difference. Whether you are a leader in your home, your church, or the marketplace, this is a must-read!"

Terry Meeuwsen, Cohost, *The 700 Club*

"If you are interested in living life with robust passion, if you are interested in leaving a legacy of compassionate service to others, if you need help implementing these desires, then read *Ten Thousand Horses*. It will inspire you and provide instruction for the journey."

Reid Carpenter, President, Leadership Foundations of America

"*Ten Thousand Horses* is a fun book to read; it provides sound leadership principles in a clear manner, but, as importantly, it illustrates the impact of leadership principles in the way we live our lives and the way our daily lives and experiences inform our leadership."

Roger A. Oxendale, President and CEO,
Children's Hospital of Pittsburgh

"*Ten Thousand Horses* offers a recipe for corporate success using universal principles in a story that is compelling, inspirational, and practical, integrating the very aspects of leadership that produce magic when aligned."

Leah Kalish, Program Director, Yoga Ed.

"Leadership is one of the toughest jobs there is. Stahl-Wert and Jennings show that by engaging the employee's mind, heart, and hands in the workplace, the 'true' leader can unleash a self-renewing wave of energy, creativity, and achievement that ultimately results in a vastly improved bottom line. Enjoy this book. Reflect on its teachings. But, most importantly, use its age-old wisdom and make a difference in your life and the lives of people you affect."

Stan Geyer, former Chairman and CEO, Entegris, Inc.

"Using fiction to reveal the facts about human capacity building, Stahl-Wert and Jennings expose the myth that leadership is merely 'what one does.' Leadership involves everything that you are. This story is a one-session read."

Bruce Bickel, Senior Vice President, PNC

"*Ten Thousand Horses* confronts your apathies, enriches your spirit, inspires your leadership desires, and warms your heart for the needs of others."

Jeff Anderson, Executive Vice President, Good News Holdings

"We put Stahl-Wert and Jennings' first book, *The Serving Leader*, to very effective use throughout our company. Their new book, *Ten Thousand Horses*, is an inspiring road map to worker engagement and will help leaders at every level to help others succeed. Read this book, and hang onto your hat!"

Paul Klaassen, Founder, Chairman, and CEO, Sunrise Senior Living

"This is a terrific book. We continue to build a high-engagement culture using practices aligned with the principles John and Ken develop in their book. And what a story! As with their last book, *The Serving Leader*, these two friends have written a story that will challenge both your heart and your mind. Thanks, guys."

Roger Marchetti, Senior Vice President, Amylin Pharmaceuticals, Inc.

"John Stahl-Wert and Ken Jennings' 'Engagement Equation' of $T \times 3C = E$ can be to business leaders what Einstein's revolutionary equation of $E = mc^2$ was to the scientific community. In *Ten Thousand Horses*, they share their innovative equation with business leaders of every type of enterprise and organization. It's an equation that is sure to get workers fully engaged with their job—and keep them engaged!"

Paul J. Meyer, Founder, Success Motivation International, Inc., and more than 40 other companies, and coauthor of the *New York Times* bestseller *Chicken Soup for the Golden Soul*

TEN
THOUSAND
HORSES

TEN THOUSAND HORSES

HOW LEADERS HARNESS
RAW POTENTIAL FOR
EXTRAORDINARY RESULTS

JOHN STAHL-WERT
KEN JENNINGS

BERRETT-KOEHLER PUBLISHERS, INC.
San Francisco

Berrett-Koehler Publishers, Inc.
235 Montgomery Street, Suite 650
San Francisco, CA 94104-2916
Tel: (415) 288-0260   Fax: (415) 362-2512   www.bkconnection.com

Ordering Information

Quantity sales. Special discounts are available on quantity purchases by corporations, associations, and others. For details, contact the "Special Sales Department" at the Berrett-Koehler address above.

Individual sales. Berrett-Koehler publications are available through most bookstores. They can also be ordered directly from Berrett-Koehler: Tel: (800) 929-2929; Fax: (802) 864-7626; www.bkconnection.com

Orders for college textbook/course adoption use. Please contact Berrett-Koehler: Tel: (800) 929-2929; Fax: (802) 864-7626.

Orders by U.S. trade bookstores and wholesalers. Please contact Ingram Publisher Services, Tel: (800) 509-4887; Fax: (800) 838-1149; E-mail: customer.service@ ingrampublisherservices.com; or visit www.ingrampublisherservices.com/Ordering for details about electronic ordering.

Printed in the United States of America

Berrett-Koehler books are printed on long-lasting acid-free paper. When it is available, we choose paper that has been manufactured by environmentally responsible processes. These may include using trees grown in sustainable forests, incorporating recycled paper, minimizing chlorine in bleaching, or recycling the energy produced at the paper mill.

Library of Congress Cataloging-in-Publication Data
Stahl-Wert, John.
    Ten thousand horses : how leaders harness raw potential for extraordinary results / John Stahl-Wert, Ken Jennings.
      p. cm.
    ISBN 978-1-57675-450-4 (hardcover)
    1. Leadership. 2. Employee motivation. 3. Management. 4. Teams in the workplace. I. Jennings, Ken (Kenneth R.) II. Title.
    HD57.7.S715   2007
    658.4'092—dc22   2007005523

FIRST EDITION
12 11 10 09 08 07   10 9 8 7 6 5 4 3 2 1

Cover design by Cassandra Chu.
Interior design and composition by Beverly Butterfield, Girl of the West Productions.
Copyediting by PeopleSpeak.

This book is dedicated to

Ed and Betty Bauman
Jim and Vicki Covey
Chris and Bonnie Cox
Ben and Sharon Dilla
Howard and Delisa Eddings
Craig and Jan Esterly
Jeanne Jennings
Russ and Doris Lloyd
Ernie and Janice Miller
Bobby and Michele Polito
Roger and Lisa Slayton
Steve and Kathy Wert
Doug and Jayne Ann Wilson
Douglas and Rebecca Thut Witmer

You will understand why.

CONTENTS

Preface ▲ *xi*

Acknowledgments ▲ *xv*

End of the Rope ▲ 1

The Climb of Trust ▲ 9

Mounting the Challenge ▲ 31

Directing the Charge ▲ 59

Leading the Cheer ▲ 87

New Engagement ▲ 109

Engagement Equation ▲ 117

Taking the Next Step ▲ 118

About the Authors ▲ *119*

These small and perishable bodies we now have were
given to us as ponies are given to schoolboys. We must learn
to manage: not that we may some day be free of horses altogether
but that some day we may ride bare-back, confident and rejoicing,
those greater mounts, those winged, shining and world-shaking
horses which perhaps even now expect us with impatience,
pawing and snorting in the King's stables.

C. S. LEWIS
Miracles

PREFACE

▲

I n our work with leaders and managers from many industries, no issue recurs with greater pain and frequency than that of worker underperformance. Every leader knows that a fully engaged employee can make an extraordinary impact on the success of the enterprise. Engaged workers show up with a committed attitude; they bring their whole selves—all their experience, talent, imagination, brains, and heart—with them to work.

The pain lies in the fact that engaged employees are the exception. The majority of workers in every business are disengaged or worse.

If you lead or manage people, you suffer from this pain. A few of your followers give it their all. Most of your workers, by contrast, are disengaged. They do the necessary minimum. They show up on time, do just what is expected, and leave on time. Far from bringing their whole selves to work, they bring what they must, and no more.

Here's what every observant leader knows: worker inattention and apathy in our enterprises result in losses of momentum and opportunity that arguably represent our number one cost of doing business.

The pain we hear about in our work with leaders and managers is the pain of what might have been—of what could be—if only more employees decided to really show up!

Significant and recent breakthroughs in management thinking have advanced our understanding of worker "engagement" and its impact on innovation, competitiveness, and profitability. When it comes to organizational results, workers who only satisfactorily comply with performance expectations bear no resemblance whatsoever to workers who actively engage themselves in the purposes and goals of their enterprise.

Research by the Gallup Organization, for example, shows that only 29 percent of workers are engaged at work (that is, they display passion for and feel connected to your company and share their ideas with you for moving the company forward). By contrast, 71 percent of workers are disengaged (they essentially sleepwalk through the day, meeting only your baseline expectations, or in the worst cases they're actively working to undermine your company's performance). Do the math: 29 percent are engaged, but you pay them all!

On the other hand, the research shows that work groups that display high levels of employee engagement produce a 44 percent higher-than-average employee retention rate, a 56 percent higher-than-average level of customer loyalty, a 50 percent higher-than-average safety record, a 50 percent higher-than-average rate of productivity, and 33 percent higher-than-average profitability.

The facts are these: worker disengagement (and worse) is omnipresent. What causes worker disengagement and what would cure it are well researched and diagnosed, but little has been done to date to translate the new findings of this research into everyday leadership and management practices.

In short, a practical guide that could be used every day for transforming a workforce into a fully engaged "achievement force" is still largely missing from the toolboxes of most leaders and managers. What is not missing is the recognition by hundreds of thousands of company, divisional, and work group leaders that the problem of worker disengagement is vast and that it costs us big time on our bottom line.

The pressures of the expanding global marketplace will only take this challenge to a new level of urgency. A fully engaged workforce fuels competitive advantage and sustainability. A future of innovation, upon which a national economy must increasingly rely, likewise requires fully engaged workers. The worker-engagement challenges that leaders and managers must face will only sharpen and intensify in years to come.

Beyond this organizational need for worker engagement is the broader societal problem that it mirrors: wasted and thrownaway human potential. Untapped human energy, passion, ideas, and talents within society represent an incalculably great and largely hidden cost to every human community. "Engagement," fully understood, is a need that touches each of us in every sphere of our lives.

We suggest you read this short story without pen and paper the first time. Take it in—its characters, story line, discoveries, and conclusions. A few charts scattered throughout will introduce the model we use for worker engagement—the Engagement Equation, as we call it—that underpins the story, but these charts will be reviewed again in full at the end, so there's no harm skimming past them. Online, a free-to-use, complete Engagement Planning Workbook will take you from this story into your own real work as a leader of others.

We also invite you to take in the aspects of this story that are more personal. Without giving away secrets from the story line, this book about engagement touches upon business-related and deeper matters in our lives as authors—matters that we care about deeply. At the most significant level, the story we bring you is true. The characters and what they experience in these pages are well known to us. While names, places, and details are fictional, we know the people in this book. It is more than likely that you know them, too.

The people who work for you, whether few or many, are capable of doing much more to advance your enterprise, for your own—as well as their own—great gain. As a matter of fact, most of them would like to *do more than they're doing, contribute more powerfully, and make a greater difference.* No kidding! For the most part, human beings carry around an unspoken yearning to get to the end of their workday—not to mention their work life—feeling that it was actually worth it.

You can make this happen! As a leader, you can make the difference that allows the folks whose paychecks you sign to make their difference. Not only can you make this happen, but as the leader, you're the one—yes, this too is verified by research—who decides whether or not it does happen. Leadership makes the difference!

May this story and the work tools that come along with it encourage and equip you to start today.

JOHN STAHL-WERT
KEN JENNINGS
Pittsburgh, Pennsylvania
April 2007

ACKNOWLEDGMENTS

▲

We would like to begin by thanking the extraordinary editorial team at Berrett-Koehler—Johanna Vondeling, Jeevan Sivasubramaniam, and Steve Piersanti—for the pleasure of doing challenging work in excellent spirit. Paraphrasing an ancient psalm, at Berrett-Koehler, "High standards and good cheer are met together, tough-mindedness and warm-heartedness have kissed each other."

Thanks for outstanding work by BK's design, production, sales, marketing, and publicity team of Rick Wilson, Dianne Platner, Kristen Frantz, María Jesús Aguiló, Michael Crowley, Robin Donovan, Ken Lupoff, Marina Cook, Tiffany Lee, Catherine Lengronne, and Ian Bach. Your skill is a tremendous gift to authors!

Sharon Goldinger at PeopleSpeak and Bev Butterfield at Girl of the West Productions again combed all the confusing tangles out of our manuscript and provided the wonderful look and design of the book.

Marcus Buckingham and the Gallup Organization did the research that undergirds our understanding of worker engagement. Stan Geyer taught us how "integrity-aligned" organizations produce cultures of full engagement. Rick Wellock guided our thinking about how human beings make progress when they learn to receive, learn to release, and learn to rejoice. The innovations in this book stand upon the foundation stones these colleagues have laid.

The reviewers made the book better. Thank you to Jim "Gus" Gustafson, Philip Heller, John Hirt, Karen Kramer Horning, Harry Howell, Jeff Icenhower, Janie Jeffers, Jeffrey Kulick, Patrick Ogburn, Barbara Schultz, and Karen Sussman for your excellent catches, suggestions, warnings, and cheers.

Scott Beilke, Bruce Bickel, Kirk Botula, Donna Brighton, Bonnie Budzowski, Lois Creamer, Sam Deep, Jim Dittmar, Darrin Grove, Glenn Main III, Diane Miller, Jerry McNellis, Abu Noaman, Raji Sankar, Randhir Setthi, Lisa Slayton, Roger Slayton, Bridget Snebold, and Joanne Spence contributed ideas, counsel, imagination, planning, and encouragement—and an abiding enthusiasm for this project. Thank you.

Matthew and David Jennings deserve particular thanks for the hand they gave in the critical early stage of the writing and editing. Take a bow, Matt and David.

Emma and Clara Stahl-Wert; David, Matthew, and Sara Jennings; and Conner Mendenhall—our children—were much in mind throughout the writing.

Love to Milonica Stahl-Wert and Heather Hyde Jennings who share in the work we do and in its pleasures.

And finally, our thanks go to God. This story about leaders and children is his story; the good in it is from him, as all good is.

Whatever's wrong with this book is our fault. No news there!

TEN
THOUSAND
HORSES

END
OF THE
ROPE

Matt James was slumped forward onto the executive conference table, his forehead pressed against the gleaming rich mahogany finish, his arms outstretched before him as though in prayer. He was alone, his mute supplication aimed at no one. His boss and the company's executive team had departed the meeting half an hour before, leaving him to ponder their ultimatum and to stare down into the depths of his ruin. They'd given him one more chance to try to light a fire under his lackluster team, and at the very end they offered him words of hope and encouragement. They were sticking with him, they had said, because they believed in him. They just knew he could turn his twenty-two-member team around, tap into "all that incredible talent" that was going to waste, and get some real results!

But Matt knew that he couldn't. He had already tried everything he could think of and had nothing to show but two years of divisional losses in advertising clients and profits. The executive team had said they believed in him, but their faces told him something else. The team's collective show of faith hadn't come easily; their smiles and affirming nods had required an obvious exercise of unwilling muscle. It wasn't that he blamed them. The truth was, he didn't believe in himself anymore.

Matt closed his eyes, letting his forehead rest more heavily on the table's surface. He'd orchestrated two downsizings in his brief, unimpressive tenure as the company's newest "rising star."

He'd brought in expert consultants and spearheaded a major strategy change—but to no effect. His division at Lumina Communications Corporation was sluggish at best. The great potential he thought he saw in his staff had not made any public appearances. It was as though they didn't care; their minimally "satisfactory" performance was no better than could be expected from a gang of clock punchers, and often it was worse.

Most troubling of all was that people in the division he'd inherited had treated him well in the beginning. They'd seemed excited about his appointment as team leader and, truth be told, had given him the benefit of the doubt—for a while.

But then their energy had waned. One by one, members of his team began to back off. Where at first they brought their whole selves to the job, now many of them seemed to bring nothing more than scraps and leftovers.

Matt's job was now on the line. Though "a final chance" had just been offered, he knew it was just the extra rope required to finish him off. There was no doubt about it, Matt concluded. He was finished.

———◆———

Seventeen hundred miles away, David Butler was absorbed in a timeless dusty dance, his cowboy boots moving with a languorous rhythm in a circle around his new partner, a highly agitated mustang stallion. David's posture and bearing were relaxed, the mustang's wary and tense. David would take a few slow steps forward along the horse's left flank, always leaving the mustang's forward path open, quietly speaking to him all the while. Whenever the horse's head and neck would crane high, ears erect, David would pause and wait for the panic to subside. If the mustang took a step or two forward, testing the openness of its path to freedom, David would move in nearly the same direction as the horse, his back turned slightly toward it, and take a few steps as though to offer leadership. "I'm not here to trap you, boy," David would say quietly. "See? I'm just moving a little ahead of you. Stay on your own course if you like, or follow mine; the choice is yours."

David and the mustang were inside a rough wooden corral surrounded by miles of high-elevation, open grassland. The snow-covered peaks of Rampart Range rose up to frame the western backdrop to this rugged scene. An intensely blue sky laden with massively brilliant clouds caused man and horse to seem small and vulnerable, too perilously exposed to nature's raw wild beauty.

"That's a good boy," David said quietly, encouragingly, when on his next lead the mustang altered his course to take a few small steps after him. "That's a good boy," he repeated. "It's a beginning!"

———◆———

In an instant, Matt James jerked up out of his seat, his body re-animating so quickly that the motion might have been caused by the yank of a puppeteer's strings. Standing erect, his shoulders squared, Matt stared out over a great distance, a new hint of possibility flickering in his gaze.

Unbidden, the face of his old mentor had appeared in his mind's eye, staring back up at him from the depths of his despair. *It's not the end, Matt,* he heard David say, the customary edge of good humor goading him to lighten up. *Not the end at all, my boy; it's a beginning.*

That's exactly what David would say, Matt mused, his con-
viction growing that he'd had an extremely good idea. His former mentor, David Butler, the now-retired celebrated corporate
turnaround specialist would say just that. Put him into the room
with almost any despairing board or executive, tell him the
plain truth of just how bad things were, and David would
shrug; smile his unperturbed, seen-it-before smile; and call it a
starting point, a place to begin.

Striding out of the conference room with renewed energy,
Matt punched the button for the forty-third floor and rode the
elevator down three levels to his divisional offices. It had been
a late-afternoon executive-team meeting, but he felt certain
Deb would still be at her desk, veteran that she was. You didn't
keep the privilege of serving a midtown Manhattan advertising
executive, even a midlevel one, by abandoning your desk before
six. More than that, though, Deb's tenure exceeded his own at
Lumina; she was one of the few left whose commitment hadn't
wavered, and he was happy he could still count on her.

"Glad you're here, Deb," Matt called out as he rounded the
corner to her section, his lanky stride unbroken. "David Butler's
an old mentor from business school. He's deep in my contacts
file somewhere, but it's been a very long time and I haven't a
clue where he's disappeared to." Matt passed Deb's desk, smiling his appreciation for her capacity to fulfill the task. "Would
you find him for me?" he asked, passing into his own office and
closing the door.

Deb found him, or rather, she found his ranch. The young-
sounding woman who answered the phone, Sara Jarrel, told her
that Mr. Butler could not be disturbed—this in spite of the air
of significance Deb had put into her appeal. "A business col-
league of Mr. Butler's," Deb had explained to the whelp. "Mr.
Matt James calling from New York City."

She may as well have tried to impress this cowpuncher with her skill at hailing cabs. "David said no calls, ma'am," Sara replied, her voice conveying a questioning tone that was aimed at Deb: *Are you getting this, Miss Tightly-Wound-Lady-from-New-York? Do you realize just how not an emergency this is?*

"We've just got in a new mustang," Sara then added, deciding to give a small additional explanation. "He's a real wild one, and they just got started. Could David call your man after dinner?" she then inquired, patiently taking down the number. "It'll be Colorado time," Sara added at the end, not certain her New York phone counterpart understood all that much about the way the real world worked.

Deb terminated the call as politely and quickly as she could to stop herself from saying something she would regret.

"And Matt, try not to forget that Mr. Butler will be calling you 'Colorado time,'" Deb had repeated very earnestly at the end of her report of the conversation, her fingers scratching quotation marks in the air, her mouth turned in the barest hint of a smile. With nothing more to report, she turned to finish her work for the day back at her desk. "Her man" would just have to handle things from here.

"Good night, Deb," Matt called after her, grinning at her recitation and at the amazing news of his old mentor. A ranch? Colorado? Wild mustangs?

That night David called Matt. They talked a long time, renewing a friendship that had meant much to Matt when he was in business school and David was an adjunct faculty member. David had taken a special interest in Matt during those earlier years, and as the younger man described in detail the problem he was facing, David quickly focused his attention.

"David, I'm up against it," Matt concluded. "I've tried everything I know, but it's not working. My tenure as a salesman was tremendously successful when it was just me on the line. Ever since my promotion, it's like a totally different game. I'm leading a team of people," he added for clarification. "The talent that's on my team looks great on paper, but our results don't show it. Potential is all I've got, truth be told. Raw potential," he qualified.

"Could you come here and help me?" he concluded, his voice a plea.

After a long silence, David finally replied, "Matt, I care about what's going on; I care about you. But I can't come to New York."

"We'll make it easy for you," Matt countered. "We'll fly you back and forth to New York; you set the schedule."

"Ease is not the issue. Here's where my work is. What we accomplish here, working with . . ." David paused, searching for words.

"Wild horses," Matt interjected, completing his former mentor's sentence. He knew what David did.

"Sure. Wild horses are a part of it," David agreed. "But what we really work with is what you just told me you work with: raw potential. What we accomplish here doesn't take place in theory. I can't do this work in principle. It happens in real time, in person. I need to be here."

Matt's slump was back. Horses! His mentor had lined up his priorities and given him a lovely position—just to the backside of a horse.

Another silence ensued. "Tell you what," David said. "Why don't you come here? On the ranch I've got the time you need. Bring your story and your questions, and I'll do the best I can for you. Then go back to New York and apply what we've discussed. If you want, come back for more. Let's see if we can get you some real results!"

It was agreed. Matt would draw up a consultant's contract, though David warned him that it was going to be an unusual engagement. Matt would learn "hands-on," as David put it, at the ranch. He'd learn by working beside David, not by sitting in a room with flip charts.

"David?" Matt asked, just before they'd hung up the phones. "What does 'hands-on' mean?" He tried to make the question sound jaunty, but the nervousness in his voice betrayed him.

David chuckled. "Just depends," he answered cryptically. "You know the expression 'hang on to your hat'? Hands are real good for that, Matt, just to give you one case in point. They're also good for holding the reins, but maybe I'm getting a little ahead of myself. Just bring your hands," David concluded. "There's a lot to touch here and a lot to love; you'll see."

THE
CLIMB
OF
TRUST

The newness of everything around him—and the strangeness of it all—made it seem to Matt that the volume button had been turned up on all his senses. Only one week had passed since he'd hung up the phone with David, one short week and then a few hours of flight. But the life he'd led seemed so distant now, the world he left a gray and shadowy place.

Matt's flight that morning to Colorado Springs had been smooth, and halfway across the small parking lot from the airport to his rental car, he had stopped, propped his wheeled suitcase against a post, and looked around. The closeness of the sky amazed him, as did its blueness and its size. He took a breath, a big breath, and then another.

He'd driven slowly, a tourist to this new world, a child on his first outing. Driving northwest out of Colorado Springs, Matt wound his way in and around the colossal burnt umber rock outcroppings of the Garden of the Gods and climbed ever higher, Pike's Peak rising to nearly three miles' elevation to the west. And then he'd found the entrance sign for "High Summit Ranch," a smaller placard reading "Wild Mustang Adoption Program." After driving up the ranch's long and winding lane, he'd been greeted with a father's embrace by David. He'd been immediately ushered into a spacious dining hall for a late private lunch and then out to the ranch's horse stables. His transfiguration from suited executive to denim-clad ranch guest had happened so quickly, and what he now stood face-to-face with threatened to overwhelm his senses altogether.

"Her name's Jessie," David was saying, cinching the girth, evidently unwavering in his expectation that Matt would momentarily mount the great steed he had just thrown a saddle on. "She's a horse," David added playfully, glancing up at Matt to read his expression.

Matt took no notice of David's look. Standing directly in front of him was a mottled red beast of such size that Matt had to look up to meet its appraising gaze.

"Ever seen a horse?" David continued.

"Course I've seen a horse," Matt gulped, realizing that his mouth had been hanging open. Slowly, he put out his hand and moved it toward the soft nose of the muscular animal that stood before him. At first touch, Jessie nickered, pressing her nose acceptingly into Matt's hand.

"It's just that I've never been this close to one," he added, remembering to breathe.

David smiled. "Jessie's one of the most gentle and forgiving horses on the ranch. And she's already added you to her list of friends. So, let's take a ride, shall we? I want to introduce you to a few people this afternoon."

There apparently being no discussion on this suggestion permitted, Matt put his foot where David pointed (a "stirrup," Matt noted, checking the little box in his brain under "stuff to learn"), grabbed fast to the hold David showed him ("pommel," check!), and hoisted himself awkwardly into the saddle. He'd heard of saddles.

Following David's brief instructions, and mimicking the actions of his mentor as best he could, Matt caused Jessie to lurch into motion behind the lead horse. He was glad David wasn't watching those first fifty yards. The "steering" on this horse seemed terribly loose to Matt; it reminded him of driving a bumper car, each effort at guidance responded to in a time-delayed and imprecise fashion.

Matt and David headed for the jagged granite cliffs rising dramatically out of the Colorado high-country terrain only a mile west of the ranch house. Along the way, David started talking.

"In my earlier business years, I was seen as very effective," David said, offering Matt nothing that he didn't already know. David's reputation for success was why Matt had sought him out, why Matt had admired him years earlier in business school, and why, indeed, the MBA program had retained David back then as an adjunct faculty member.

"I knew how to cut costs and trim head count with the best of them, and I always showed quick results on the bottom line."

Matt was listening, but the greater part of his attention was focused on staying atop his horse. The ground they were covering had turned from a smooth, even trail into an uneven, rocky path.

"At some point I began to notice, though," David continued, "as I looked in the rearview mirror, that my so-called turnarounds hadn't held up. Not long after I'd left one assignment for the next, my results started to sour, and the gains I had achieved began to unravel. It happened every time, Matt! The business press made me famous because their attention span was too short. In truth, my so-called results were largely smoke and mirrors."

Matt's attention shifted back to David. The pathway their horses were following was steadily worsening, but now it was David's remarks that posed the greater threat to Matt. Jessie came to a sudden standstill, Matt unaware of having done anything to cause her halt.

David brought his own horse to a stop and turned to check on his friend. Matt could not wipe the apprehension off his face as he looked at the man who was supposed to be his answer.

"Not only were my so-called turnarounds short-lived, Matt," David continued mercilessly, shifting his weight in the saddle to fully face the younger man, "but they hurt a lot of people." David had not missed the reason Matt brought his horse unwittingly to a standstill. He had intended, in fact, to start this "consultation" on just this point and knew it would violate his client's expectations.

"And I thought nothing of it then, or I should say that I thought this was the mark of a good turnaround. If my efforts didn't hurt people, then I wasn't doing it right. I actually believed that."

Matt observed that David was not exactly as he remembered him. He was older, of course, and Matt quickly did the math to confirm the surprising fact that twenty years had passed since they had last been together. Realizing this, Matt crunched yet another number; since David was twenty years his senior, the mentor he remembered had been the very age he was now. This little mathematical fact—coupled with the confession David was in the middle of making and the ineptitude Matt felt sitting astride this horse—created the beginnings of a darkened mood in Matthew James.

How could the heroic businessman David Butler have been only forty-seven years old back when he had then seemed so seasoned, such a veteran, so wise? Worse, why did his own forty-seven years provide him with none of these advantages?

"I'll tell you this, my friend," David was saying, his gaze steady, his eyes kind. "When we believe that we're the savior of the day, that's when we're the most lost of all." He let the point hang in the air for a moment and then grinned. "I'm gettin' ahead of myself. C'mon. I can show you what I mean a whole lot more effectively than I can talk about it."

And with that, David pressed his horse into motion, his pace now faster than before they had stopped. Matt "giddy-apped" Jessie, pressed his heels in against her flanks as he had seen done so many times in the movies, and hoped the horse would comply.

This was not the same man he had previously known, Matt realized. There was a kind of sadness about him now, it seemed to Matt, or if not sadness, then reserve. The gregarious and often aggressive edge he remembered from years earlier had been replaced by something more sober, more reflective, or more serene.

"You said you began to notice that the turnarounds didn't last," Matt called after his mentor. "What happened? I mean," he stammered, not quite sure where he was going with this question, "did you figure out why? You must have," he pressed, a small note of desperation in his voice. "The articles I read about you couldn't be all wrong."

The path widened for a stretch, and Jessie pulled forward to keep pace with her fellow horse, the two riders now nearly side by side. The older man rode in silence, his head bowed, his shoulders slightly stooped, as though the question had placed a weight on his back.

"A moment ago I told you we're in danger when we believe we're the savior of the day," he said, looking over at Matt, his voice as serious as a storm. "So add this to the list of dangers. Don't believe your press. What you need to succeed won't come to you in the nice write-up you get in *Forbes*."

"But what exactly did you do?" Matt quickly countered, feeling a growing exasperation that his "savior" wasn't in a hurry to do any saving.

"We'll get into that, my friend," David replied, his voice lighter. "Let me just say that what I learned turned my whole model of leadership upside-down. Which is a sideways way of saying that I got my life turned upside-down," David added, looking back at Matt over his shoulder, his eyes creased with a kind smile. "Hiya!" he then barked, sending his mount instantly forward at an even quicker pace. Miraculously, Jessie followed suit, somehow discerning that the random, jerky motions taking place on her back just then did not contraindicate keeping pace with her buddy.

Matt glanced up from the saddle's pommel he was holding in a death grip. The ground blurred past him like the torrent of a fast river. Fighting the wave of dizziness this view brought upon him, he looked up, startled to see how very close they were to the sheer granite rock face before them.

"These horses sure can move," he commented, trying to impose some calm upon his uncalm self.

The corners of David's mouth crept up into a grin. He knew what Matt was feeling and remembered his own similar fears a few years ago. "You're doing well, my boy," he called back, keeping his face forward to conceal the mirth it revealed. Matt would think he was being laughed at, which wasn't the case.

Faint shouts could be heard from up ahead as the two riders approached their destination. As they came closer, the loudest of the shouts was joined by the ever-growing sound of yelling, whistling, and clapping. By the time the cliffs were only a few hundred feet away, David and Matt were engulfed in a symphony of cheers and laughter. Matt had not seen this many teenagers congregated in the same place since high school, and he glanced questioningly at David.

The drive to the Ranch had been solitary, the dining hall had been deserted, and the ride had been uninterrupted. He had expected horses, and some cowboys, surely. But teenagers? And these particular ones? The diversity of the group was astounding—Anglo, Asian, African American, and Latino all mixed up—but this was no United Nations Honors Club. One young man in particular caught Matt's attention as he and David rode up. The teenager had a tight line of earrings running along the edge of one ear, as well as several other pins and posts at his eyebrow and on his nose. His T-shirt read, "Body Piercing Saved My Life!" Matt read the young man's shirt twice, just to be sure he'd read it accurately. He had, though the sense of it escaped him entirely.

"Howyadoin'?" the young man asked, flashing Matt a bright smile as they passed.

"Doing good, thanks." Matt answered, returning the smile. *The facade is tough,* Matt mused, *but the inside isn't.*

"What's going on?" Matt asked, directing his question to David.

"It looks like we just caught the tail end of this group's rock climb. The team leader of this exercise," David continued, pointing to a tall, well-built man around whom everyone was gathered, "is the first person I wanted you to meet."

Matt's eyes roved over the group of climbers and quickly found the bright-faced man David was pointing out. His radiant smile could easily be seen from where Matt and David were standing, still fifty yards back.

"That's John Butler," David continued, a twinkle in his eye showing that he was ready for Matt's double take. "Coincidence on the last names, huh?" he said, still smiling. Matt nodded his head, his eyes showing bewilderment. "I really can't say

I've ever met anyone quite like him. Come on," he urged, dismounting and steering them both toward the circle of youths.

"Way to go, everyone," John was saying, his voice booming. "We did it. We did it together," he added for emphasis.

"John's a remarkable leader, Matt," David interjected quietly as they approached the group. "Today I'm introducing you to what we call the Ropes Course, not 'ropes' literally, though on this day we do use actual ropes. Our Ropes Course is about learning the ropes of the whole program. It's our first unit of study. John's your living lesson," he added, and then plowed forward into the group.

"What did you learn?" John asked. "Anybody want to go first?" He cocked his head toward the group, the motion reminding Matt of a bird turning its head back and forth to pick up the minutest of sounds.

"I'll go," came a voice from the back.

"Great, Mary, you start."

"I learned that the easiest-looking path is not necessarily the best. I'll also trust Bobby's instincts with the route next time." There were some pats on the back of a young man to the left of the leader and a general murmur of approval around the blushing, skinny boy in question. At the sound, John's head cocked left, his smile broadened, and his fist went in the air.

"Bobby, my man!" he crowed, pumping his fist in affirmation. "You've got the eyes of an eagle," he added.

And with this comment, Matt saw what he had been missing. John found whomever he was addressing with his ears, and while he then also pointed his gaze in that direction, his eyes remained restless, never locking in precisely on the person he was speaking with. The rock-climbing instructor was blind!

"Who's next?" John continued.

"I learned that I'm no good at rock climbing." Matt saw that this comment came from a nine- or ten-year-old boy standing with his hands in his pockets, looking like he didn't get outside much. His hair was a jet-black tangled mess, perhaps painstakingly put that way. His skin was pasty white, and he was squinting into the sun. Something about the boy—the tousled hair, the wary face, the penetrating eyes—pulled at Matt.

"What about brave enough to try something that scares you sick, Tyler?" John asked, his smile broader than ever.

"Yeah, I guess," Tyler said, looking down.

"Were you scared sick, Tyler?" John pressed.

"Yeah," Tyler answered uncomfortably.

"And did you push yourself off the edge of that cliff a few minutes ago?"

"Yeah, I did," Tyler answered, his head lifting perceptibly.

"Therefore, no guesswork needed, Tyler. You've got the heart of a lion. The fact's been established."

Another round of cheers rose up, accompanied by pats on Tyler's back. The boy was standing noticeably taller at the end of this exchange, his eyes just as intense as before but now holding an extra spark. Matt took it all in.

"I want to introduce an old friend, John," David interrupted.

"Hey, boss," John responded. "I heard you coming."

Matt doubted that someone could have heard them coming, with all the shouts and noise.

"And I was wondering who the tenderfoot was that you had with you. Jessie's quite a sweet ride, isn't she?" John added, cocking his head back and forth, casting his sightless eyes in close vicinity to where David, and presumably also the guest, stood.

Now Matt was perplexed. Could this blind man identify the sounds of individual horses, too?

"Everybody," David said loudly, "say hello to my friend Matt James."

"Hey, Matt," chorused the dozen or so youths standing around them.

"I talked to a lady in your office," exclaimed a teenage girl standing just a few feet away, her voice excited. "You made it," she added, sounding almost surprised. "My name's Sara," the teenager added, sauntering over in three lanky strides to shake Matt's hand.

"And you made a special impression on my executive assistant," Matt replied as he shook Sara's hand, chuckling at the reminder of Deb's report of her exchange with this very young woman. She couldn't be even sixteen years old, Matt observed, as Sara quickly stepped back from the greeting. Her face still held a child's roundness, he noticed, and yet her eyes betrayed that impression. It was as though she were a veteran soldier, and the watch she kept was for the next sorrow, sure to come.

"Matt is going to be spending a little time with us here, learning how we operate," David said, "and today is lesson number one."

"John," he continued, "would you say a few words to Matt about the purpose of this climbing exercise today and how it fits into the way we go about our work here?"

"What we did today, Matt," John began, "was a teaching climb. We took the entire group to the top and then rappelled back down to the bottom. All the way, I taught technique, strategy, and teamwork. We were just starting a discussion on lessons learned, including a critique of my teaching."

"Why don't you go ahead with that, John," David suggested.

"Will do," John replied, turning back to the youths standing around him. "Let's start with you, Bobby."

"Well, this was my first climb," Bobby began. "One of the things I liked was the way you shared the decision making with everyone." He paused to collect his thoughts. "I didn't know how you'd teach us anything without being able to see. But that made it even better because you made the rest of us see what you couldn't." Bobby paused again, thinking through his point. "You had to trust us," he added. "That was great," he concluded.

"I like how you made us look after each other," another girl added.

"Say more, Michelle," John urged.

"Well, you had us check each other's equipment as well as our own. And then you had us explain to each other and to you how we did the check. That really locked it in for me."

"Give Matt the big picture, John," David interrupted. "What are you trying to accomplish at this point of the training?"

"Happy to," John said, turning back toward David and Matt. "Our climb today was the result of hours of planning together, but it was only a first step in the journey. We lay out a full eighteen-month program of leadership training, Matt, which I'm sure David will show you. And we do it in groups called cohorts. We started this new cohort just three weeks ago, and we're still on the introductory unit of study—the Ropes Course."

"So, what do you teach in the Ropes Course?" Matt asked, hoping John knew the question was for him, not David.

"Think about it for a second," John replied without hesitation. "What could you learn from a blind rock-climbing instructor?"

"Um, I guess I could learn that a teacher sometimes needs to take instruction," Matt offered uncertainly.

"You could learn how to take my instruction. Remember, *I* do the teaching here," John pointed out. A few chuckles could be heard around the circle, but though Matt felt that he had just been gently scolded, John's smile hadn't wavered for a second.

"But what could you learn by considering what I must do *in order* to be an effective rock-climbing instructor?" John pressed. "What did you hear Bobby and Michelle just talk about? Remember, it's not so much that I can't see where to put my own hands and feet—I can feel my way quite excellently. More importantly, I can't see what my students are doing—I can't see whether they're learning what I'm trying to teach them. And I can't see on ahead in the climb, that is, beyond what I can feel with my own hands and feet."

"Ah!" Matt exclaimed. "I would say, then, that I could learn that there must be a great deal of information exchange," he said, more confident in this answer. "You have to be provided what you can't provide for yourself. You can't take anything for granted, and so you have to communicate more."

"True enough," John responded. "Sticking with your point for a second, would you say that under more normal circumstances, having lots of communication wouldn't really matter as much? If I could see with my own eyes, then I could take a lot more for granted and forgo the extra effort at communication?" John's smile remained strong and bright as he waited for his newest student's reply.

The question hit home. Matt's eyes went unfocused for a second as he considered how on target John's remark was. He did take a lot for granted. He would offer one of his staff only a quick explanation or orientation and then watch to see if he or she fulfilled the task or fell down. He'd thought of this as a way to test performance—whether his people were committed or talented. He had never thought that this way of leading might show that he was the one who was underperforming.

"I'm wondering," Matt said, his voice subdued, "if my team back in New York understands what I assume they understand. Mostly, I assume that staff who don't perform the way I expect know what I expect, or how to do what I expect. I assume that when they screw up, it's their fault."

"It could be their fault," John offered.

"Yeah," Matt countered, speaking more reflectively, "but more likely it's mine. They might not understand what I think I've told them."

"All right, then. Your point's established," John said. "We undercommunicate. Your New York team maybe doesn't have a clear understanding of your expectations or your plans or your strategy. And rock climbing definitely demands clarity in the communication department.

"But communication wasn't our lesson today, not at the deepest level," John pressed on. "Tyler!" he called out, turning back in the direction where the boy had earlier stood.

"Yeah?" the boy answered quietly.

"Did you step off that cliff because I did a great job of explaining how to do it?"

Tyler's eyes shifted back and forth between John and Matt. He was looking for clues about what to say, what was expected, or whether this was a trap. "You did a good job of explaining everything," he ventured, testing the water.

"Thank you, Tyler," John replied sincerely. "And was my good explanation why you had the courage to step off the side of that rock?"

Tyler's head shook back and forth, a small involuntary gesture that indicated he'd answered the question for himself. John waited.

"You were with me," Tyler said, his voice even quieter.

Matt thought that John's smile no longer seemed broad—
it was but deep. His eyes were bright. "And where was I, Tyler,
when I was with you?"

"You were off the edge of the cliff already, a couple of feet
down, waiting for me." Tyler knew this answer was correct. It's
where John was.

Instead of saying more to Tyler, John simply turned his satisfied gaze back to where David had been standing. *Mission
accomplished, boss,* his gesture said. *Take it away!*

"Well done, Tyler," David said, putting the capstone on this
exchange between the boy and John. "Carry on, friends," he
said, excusing both himself and Matt from the circle. "And
thanks for the instruction, John," he added in conclusion.

"As always, the thanks is mine, boss," John replied. "My
debt to you can never be repaid. You know that."

"Quite the other way around, in my opinion, John," David
responded quietly.

The ride back to the ranch passed quickly. Matt was deep
in thought, and David rode silently in front, offering his
younger friend some time to ponder what had just transpired.
He knew they'd be able to more easily talk about what they had
just experienced back in his office.

"You give these kids a training program in leadership," Matt
said, repeating what David had said back at the cliff side. "And
what I saw today was part of that program." David had guided
Matt into his office's conference area and settled them into
comfortable chairs.

"There's a switch inside every person, Matt," David replied.
"The 'off' position is 'I'll maybe do what I'm told while you're

watching me. But when you're not watching me, I'll do less than I'm told and maybe worse.' The 'on' position is 'I'll do everything I possibly can to make a positive contribution. I'll do it whether you're watching or not.'"

Matt was staring at David. Again he was thinking about his team back home. Deb's switch was in the "on" position, though he couldn't explain why. His leading salesman, Randy, had started out totally committed, just as Deb still was, but Randy's switch was now "off," as were those of the majority of the rest of his team. How David had gotten to this topic from the rock climb, he didn't know.

"What we're teaching is how to lead in such a way that the switch gets flipped from off to on. From apathy to investment. From 'It's not my job' to 'I'll do it.' From 'It's not my fault' to 'I'll take responsibility.' So, yes, we teach leadership, and today was part of the lesson."

"And the point of today was that I should communicate more and go over the face of the cliff first," Matt pressed on, now showing his growing irritation. He was lost. They'd left the rock face immediately after the interchange between John and Tyler as if what any of it was supposed to mean was obvious. It wasn't obvious at all—not to Matt—and he was feeling peevish.

"Let's stick to this point for another second, Matt," David added, seeing Matt's consternation. "Of course communication matters, but the Ropes Course, including today's lesson, teaches that it's about much more than words. There are actions you must take—daily, disciplined, consistent actions—if you want your team to really lock into what you're wanting and where you're going."

"I'm taking action," Matt protested, his confusion escalating.

David held his younger friend's gaze for a second. He wanted to slow Matt down and allow a moment for absorption of his words.

"Yes, Matt, you've taken action, and no, you haven't communicated enough, and yes, you're going to have to communicate more, but no, you haven't been taking the *right* actions." David was smiling kindly as he spoke to his unhappy charge, aware of the riddle he was spinning. "And I'm going to straighten you out on each one of these scores if you'll give me a chance."

Matt looked dubious and just shrugged. It wasn't like there was a Plan B.

"You like it straight. So here it is—straight. First, we teach these youths about the kind of young men and women they must be if they want to be leaders people will follow. This is personal character stuff and personal character comes *before* professional capability. Always!"

"Sounds vague," Matt replied, his tone less sharp than his point, "which is maybe why business school skipped the character subject in favor of teaching the harder capability subjects."

"Right! Character stuff is too vague and too soft," David chimed in, his voice now the one that sounded peeved, "which is total bull, by the way." David put more bite into this remark than any Matt had yet heard.

"What we teach is not vague, and it's anything but soft. And I must also tell you that there's a faith dimension to our work here with the youth. I don't want you to be blindsided by it because you're going to bump into it. But regardless of your views about faith, the character piece is vital to our program. What we mean by character is very precise and very tough-minded. The problem with teaching about character, you see, is that you have to have it first.

"And beyond the character piece, Matt," David pressed on, taking a breath, "we teach three key capabilities a leader must practice every day to get great results from a team of workers." David took another big breath and smiled an apology to his former student for the rise in emotional temperature.

"So you're saying," Matt interjected, "that great results require learning how to flip that magic switch from off to on."

David got to his feet and retrieved a legal pad off his desk, quickly scribbled something onto it and then tore off the sheet. Returning to his seat, he handed Matt the paper. It read

$$T \times 3C = E$$

"I wasn't going to give this to you up front like this. I always prefer show over tell, but I think you're not liking my experiential teaching methods all that much," he added, smiling down at his friend.

Matt grinned and waved his hand in protest.

"This is our Engagement Equation," David continued. "The E at the end of our equation stands for engagement. It refers to the switch in the 'on' position. According to research, less than a third of American workers are engaged at work. So about three out of ten workers have the switch flipped 'on.' They're there to make a difference. They bring their whole selves with them to work every day. Three out of ten, Matt! So you're hardly alone in your problem. More than two-thirds of the workforce show up with their switch in the 'off' position, or worse. Every single one of them expects to get their regular paycheck, of course," David added in deadpan.

Matt nodded his understanding.

"The $3C$ in the middle of our equation refers to three capabilities that we teach," David continued. "You and I aren't going to start into the $3C$ piece until tomorrow, so don't push me," he added playfully.

"And the T?" Matt asked.

"The T is the character piece. Go back to the cliff face. Why did Tyler take that frightening step off the top of a sheer mountain?"

"Well, I suppose because he trusted John. Tyler said it was because John was there with him. John had gone first and Tyler was to follow."

"Right," David picked up the thread of the conversation. "Trust is what the leader gains by being trustworthy, by matching actions to words. We talk about 'the say-do gap,' and it's the leader's job to close it."

"Trust," Matt repeated. "The T stands for trust."

"So our Engagement Equation begins with trust. And now I can make a point I couldn't earlier. As important as communication is, and as rampant as the problem of undercommunication is, trust is the real issue. What do you get by communicating more if your followers don't believe that your message means anything?" David gave Matt a moment to take in the point.

"And so we start with trust. Do what you promise. Is that too vague for you? Be what you ask others to be. If you've got a gap between your say and your do, nothing else you bring to the table will make enough of a difference. This is foundational, like needing good nutrition if you're going to train to become a high-performance athlete: $3C$ is the training; T is the nutrition. It begins with trust, Matt," David concluded. "It begins with character."

Matt thought about his New York team again. Did his team trust him? More specifically, did he follow through with what he promised? Was he trustworthy? He tried to be honest, certainly, but David was leading him to think about something deeper than honesty. Were his daily actions disciplined and consistent? Was he trustworthy that way?

Matt recalled an incident the prior week when he'd reversed himself on the decision to appoint Molly, once his star in sales, to the Gramming account. His reconsideration was motivated by the thought that giving this account to Randy might boost his morale, not to mention the fact that right after first telling Molly that she'd get the account, she missed a delivery schedule on another project.

When he pulled her from the new assignment, Molly's face had achieved a new registry on the hardness scale—no surprise to Matt—but Randy had received the news of his new opportunity with an equally grim face. "Sure, boss," was all he'd said.

Matt had thought this unhappiness was caused by ingratitude on Randy's part or a loss of drive. Now it occurred to him that it might have been the reversal itself that generated it. *Were there a lot of these?* he wondered. Immediately he knew the answer was yes. He'd made a lot of about-faces in his leadership always because he felt he had to. His employees weren't going to push themselves off the edge of the cliff for him, he realized. They couldn't be sure he'd be there waiting for them as he'd promised.

"How long does it take to get people to trust you?" Matt asked, his own face now grim. He knew it was a foolish question; of course, it took a long time. But he didn't feel he had a long time.

"You've got the time, Matt," David said warmly. "One of the paradoxes of leadership is that speed can really slow you down."

"Got it," Matt answered. It had taken him two years in his new executive assignment to create the crisis he was in. He could afford at least a second day to try to get out of it.

"It's dinnertime," David added, smiling. "That ride gave me an appetite. Let's go join in, shall we?"

"By the way, David," Matt spoke as they strolled across the courtyard separating David's office from the common dining hall. "I wanted to ask you where the teenagers came from. And John. What's his story?"

"This is an adoption ranch, Matt," David replied.

"Mustang adoption," Matt responded. "I know that. It's on your sign."

"Yes, mustang adoption. But people adoption, too. Every child here is in the foster care system or otherwise a ward of the state."

Matt's jaw dropped.

"We take ten new kids every six months, and the program is eighteen months long, so we've always got thirty kids in the program. Plus we often invite a few to stay on and help us run things.

"John came to us ten years ago after getting aged out."

"Aged out?" Matt probed.

"He turned eighteen without ever having been adopted. John was a foster care kid from the day of his birth to his eighteenth year. No one ever chose to make him their son. It happens a lot."

"What's a lot?" Matt asked, stopping in the middle of the courtyard.

David replied soberly, "Every time we welcome ten new kids into this program, ten thousand eighteen-year-olds age out of the foster care system never having become someone's son or daughter, never having a permanent father or mother, never living as a permanent member of a family. Every six months, ten thousand are tossed out of the system to fend for themselves. Is that a lot?" he asked.

"God!" Matt exclaimed.

"Not God's fault," David retorted, "and that doesn't count the unadopted seventeen-, sixteen-, fifteen-, fourteen-year-olds, and thirteen-year-olds. I could count on down, but it just gets more painful," he added.

Matt shook his head, looking at his mentor with astonishment.

"Mostly we only take kids younger than John, as young as nine or ten and as old as fourteen or fifteen. But John was special, and I bent the rules. And how glad I am that I did.

"C'mon," David put an arm around Matt's shoulder, reasserting his fatherly presence. "Let's have some chow."

Matt nodded and stepped into the dining hall. A quick glance told him that some thirty or forty teenagers filled the room, along with maybe two dozen adults he assumed were staff—ranch hands and trainers. But his eyes stayed on the youths. An adoption ranch. A roomful of young teenagers who needed families.

A delicious aroma of barbecued steak greeted Matt, along with the sight of steaming bowls of baked potatoes, fresh green asparagus, assortments of sauces and toppings, fresh baked bread, and jars of deep red jelly. But none of it reached him. These teens didn't have moms and dads, and in his stomach he felt nothing but a fist.

MOUNTING THE CHALLENGE

Matt's eyes opened with a start, his body electrified by the sound of a cry he was sure had been real. He'd just been dreaming that he was searching for a child who was lost, and in his dreams he had heard the child—a son—calling for help. But the cry that awakened him was surely not from his dream; it was too vivid and startling to be a dream, and it had punched a lucid hole right into the heart of his hazy, half-volume dream of searching and loss.

His eyes wide open now, he couldn't see a thing. The bright digital bedside clock wasn't shining out the time from its customary place to his right. And the light from the streetlamp outside his bedroom window was gone, the window itself indiscernible in the blackness that surrounded him. Stranger still, Matt couldn't hear anything—no horns, no buses, no sirens, no screeching brakes, no air conditioners thrumming like a plague of locusts.

And no one crying.

Matt reached to his left, feeling for the warmth of his wife asleep beside him. He was alone—lying in a narrow single bed—and realizing this, he remembered where he was. The reaching motion made his body complain loudly from a great number of muscle groups. He grimaced and recalled the awkward and jarring blows he'd taken atop a horse the day before. His chest felt heavy, too, the thin air adding its own toll to his weariness.

31

Pressing the light on the rim of his wristwatch, Matt saw that it was 3:30 a.m., 5:30 according to his body's New York clock. Alice would already be stirring, the demands as a new partner in her firm impelling her out of their bed ever earlier and bringing her home again ever later.

Matt settled back into the comfort of the mattress and covers, relieved to know that, for two more hours, nothing was pressing. The worries he left behind in New York—work worries and more personal ones—would have to wait. The bad dream that had startled him awake was just that, a dream. And the several dozen youths whose life circumstances had touched his heart the evening before would also have to wait. Resolved to do his best to push it all away for at least two more hours, Matt closed his eyes and concentrated on his breathing, willing himself to settle back toward sleep.

A young boy's voice cried out, the sound identical to the one that moments before had pushed through his dreams and pulled him up to the surface of consciousness. Matt was out of his bed in a single move, but then he paused, unsure what he should do next. No word had been spoken. The boy hadn't cried out for help, but it was as though he had. What Matt heard was the call of a son, the need of a boy somewhere in this vast house for his daddy.

He fumbled around his bedside, found the lamp, and pulled a chain that filled his room with soft light. And then he moved to the door, ready to go farther. Other doors could be heard opening and closing beyond his own, other voices speaking kindly and softly to the boy. And then the voice of his friend David reached him—not the words but the soft soothing tones of a man giving comfort. A plaintive boy's voice responded, also indecipherable, the tones tearful.

Matt stood transfixed—his hand on the knob—inside his bedroom listening to the sacred and timeless exchange of a son's pouring out his heart and a father's receiving the tears of his child and giving comfort and understanding. The voices soon receded, and doors again closed, removing the sounds of this poignant drama beyond his hearing altogether.

Matt wished he had been the one offering those tender words and gestures of comfort. Reflecting further, he realized that he would also like to have been the one receiving them. He had been dreaming that his child was lost—and, indeed, the son that was the subject of his recurring nightmare *was* lost—but Matt felt that he was the lost one. He was the one left alone. The young boy down the hall had expressed what was true for him.

"Come on in, Matt," David beckoned, gesturing for his friend to join him in the spacious dining room, where he sat at a table with a small group of his staff. "Join us," he said, handing Matt a steaming mug of very dark, heavy-looking coffee. "It's not Starbucks," he added. "We need *strong* coffee here."

"Hey, Matt," John said, the rock-climbing instructor's bright face connecting warmly with Matt.

"Good morning, John," Matt replied. "Good morning, everybody," he added.

"We're just finishing up our weekly staff leadership meeting," David said, "and given what we discussed yesterday about the say-do gap, it shouldn't surprise you to know that we use the same Engagement Equation in our leadership team that we teach to the youths."

Matt acknowledged David's remark with a nod of his head, took a seat with the assemblage of men and women at the table, and slurped a mouthful of the hottest, strongest, blackest coffee he had ever tasted. "Do you mind if I take some notes?" Matt asked, his voice straining against an overwhelming impulse to cough, his eyes tearing from the burning taste of the scalding brew. "It'd help me out," he added, carefully placing his coffee mug onto the table before him, the gesture resembling that of a hazmat specialist disposing of volatile toxic waste.

"Write away," a boyish-looking young cowboy pitched in, his eyes twinkling at Matt's reaction to the coffee. "That's what we do here: help each other a little further down the trail. I'm Teddy," he added.

"Thanks, Teddy," Matt nodded, doing his best to erase the remainder of the grimace from his face.

"Actually, we only have a few minutes, Matt," David interjected, "but why doesn't someone say a quick word to my friend about our 'great purpose' here. What is the great purpose of the ranch and its leadership team?"

"I'll start," the young cowboy replied. "You wouldn't guess it to see me here, but my degree's from Harvard, and as great as that was, nothing's helped me more than what I learned here about the daily discipline of anchoring every goal, every plan, and every decision to our great purpose. We stress the importance of purpose-aligned goals, purpose-aligned plans, and purpose-aligned decisions. When I say this out loud, it sounds obvious. But vision statements are famous for living in drawers. Our great purpose lives in daily discipline."

Matt looked at the young man with a curious expression. Every impression was of a cowboy: dress, slouch, twang. There was nothing "Hahvahd" about Teddy.

"What we're all about is providing the lost children of our society with a vehicle that delivers them to a lifetime of full engagement and meaningful achievement," the ex-Harvard boy declared. "Our great purpose is 'Every Child a Hope, Every Child a Home.'"

The second Matt heard Teddy's words, he believed them. He believed in them. It was as though he'd just heard the words he'd been searching for. Every child is a hope, and every child needs a home. He could think of nothing more urgent, more important, than giving himself to these words.

"Would you tell me about the ranch?" Matt pressed. He knew that David wanted to move on, but he wanted to hear more. "I don't mean the ranch itself," he added. "I mean the ranch and the children. How did you turn a horse ranch into a ranch for kids?"

"The simplest answer," David interjected, "is that we didn't. I assure you, we never saw this coming. We were training wild mustangs for adoption. Then some things happened in my life." David paused, looking now at his hands clasped on the tabletop. Then he cleared his throat.

"And then other things happened," he continued, shrugging his shoulders, his eyes now very soft. "Life's funny," he added, glancing up at Matt, his face devoid of humor. "Now's not really the time for all that, though," he added, smiling his apology for the unanswered questions, not to mention the new ones his behavior had raised. "I'm more interested in show than tell, as I've told you. So, if you don't mind," he concluded, rising to his feet and gesturing with a wag of his head for Matt to come along.

"Show's good," Matt answered, matching his mentor's kindness. "Let's go see."

David's face was suffused with warmth. His eyes swept the staff circle—his appreciation of them could not have been communicated more effectively.

"We're headed to the stables, Matt," David added, turning toward the door. Matt fell in beside the older man while the staff efficiently—contentedly—dispersed to their day's incredible duties.

———•◦•◦◦———

"I could start the story by telling you what's wrong with the kids we serve," David said. They were walking across a wide, grassy field, heading toward stables in the direction of the snow-crusted peaks to the west. Matt could see the long, low stabling area with several vast rectangular corrals stretching out to the north and south, as well as several smaller circular corrals, one of which was the focus of a great deal of attention at the moment. Ranch hands and some kids stood next to or sat on the perimeter fence, and a horse and girl could be seen within the circle.

"It's where the turnaround specialist starts," David continued, never breaking stride.

"Excuse me?" Matt replied. His mind had drifted. They'd been talking about kids, and he'd been watching the circular path of the horse and girl as David and he closed the several-hundred-yard gap between them and the stables. The field they were crossing required some attention, too, what with the patchy tufts of sharp, course grass that had to be sidestepped and the additional hazards deposited here and there by the ranch's several-dozen horses. A stroll up Winged Foot's storied eighteenth fairway this wasn't.

"Starting with what's wrong," David repeated. "I just said that that's the way the turnaround specialist would do it." His voice sounded impatient; his student wasn't paying attention.

"Well . . ." Matt stammered, "it's why you need a turnaround, isn't it? Something's wrong, obviously." Matt was suddenly feeling impatient again. And he was paying full attention. Wasn't the fact that something was terribly wrong the reason, indeed, that he was tromping across this unkempt field in the first place?

David chuckled. The tension that suddenly seized his younger friend reminded him to let go of his own. He gave Matt a slap on the back.

"It's why you need a turnaround," David answered affirmingly, encouragingly. "Something's wrong. But when it comes to *addressing* what's wrong, you need a very different starting point."

Matt walked a few paces in silence. If the fact that something's wrong triggers the need for a turnaround, he was thinking, then why isn't the fact that something's wrong the starting point for fixing it?

"So, as I say," David resumed, his voice now relaxed and unperturbed, "I could start the story by telling you what's wrong with the kids we serve. And there's plenty wrong, as you say. Plenty wrong," he repeated, his voice quieter.

"But it's not the right place to start. It never is." David let the point hang in the air for a moment before continuing.

"Around here, we start with what's right. And the good news is that there's always also plenty that's right," he added emphatically.

"Please explain," Matt implored. "There's a problem, but you don't deal with it?"

"Hold up here, Matt," David said, his voice now stern. "You and I aren't having the same conversation. I'm talking about these children—I want you to understand how we flip the switch that brings these children back to life, how we move them from disengaged to engaged. But you're talking about yourself—you want me to teach you how to achieve a turn-around back in New York." David stood eye to eye with Matt, his words effectively drawing a line in the dirt right where they stood.

"Did I miss something, David?" Matt replied, the edge of frustration in his voice sharpening. "Didn't I come here so you could help me?"

David's eyes softened. "You did. And I promise to do my very best to help you, Son," he replied. "On whose terms do you want that help?"

Matt lowered his gaze. His mentor had challenged him for position. And won. He, Matt, wasn't here to call the shots, was he? So why was he even trying? And, furthermore, David had called him "Son," a title of junior rank, which he deserved and, coming from his friend, liked.

"Your terms, David," Matt answered, again meeting David's gaze. "I agreed to your terms on this consultation from the start, so I'm good to go with that."

"My suggestion is that you receive help on the terms that are available, which, by the way, are neither yours nor mine. I've found it works better that way." David's smile was broad, his eyes creased with kindness.

"Now the fact of the matter is," David continued, putting his arm across the shoulder of his new charge and steering him onward toward the corral, "that the best way I know to help you is to show you how we help these kids. Better still," he added, "let's get you involved with helping them, too."

"I'd like that," Matt answered, his voice firm.

"I told you yesterday that today I'd introduce you to the capabilities we teach in our model. There are three of them." David opened the gate in the outer fencing so they could go inside the stabling area. Within the perimeter fence stood the long, red stables for the horses; a taller barn at the end of the stables whose doors were open to reveal great stacks of hay bales; and several small, interior, white-fenced ovals, one of which was their obvious destination.

"In your case," David continued, "you can just as well think of the three *C*s in our Engagement Equation as a three-part capability map for a successful turnaround. The biggest myth that needs to be busted is that turning something from bad to good is somehow different from turning something from good to great. It's the very same deal, Matt. I didn't used to know that."

With that, David moved past Matt, striding toward the action in the central oval. Matt followed, pondering David's final, cryptic remark. *It's the very same deal?* If you're starting out with something that isn't working, surely you have to do things differently than if you're starting out with something that is working. It only stood to reason.

"I want you to spend some time this morning with Sara Jarrel," David said, interrupting Matt's train of thought. They stepped up against the corral fence. "You met her at the rock climb yesterday, and she'll give you a great, practical understanding of the next part of our Engagement Equation."

Matt now saw that the girl inside the corral, her face nearly hidden by a great cowboy hat, was, indeed, Sara. The thought of spending time with her pleased him immensely; her tough act had gotten his attention. But there was something more, something beneath the swagger, that had captured his heart. Whatever she'd been through that caused her to be on a constant vigil for disappointment had not snuffed out her longing for something good. This girl might have missed the experience of childhood, but in the hopefulness that peeked out from behind her guard, Matt could still discern the child.

He looked down at his boots. Thinking about Sara, he realized, had caused him to think about himself. She made an excellent mirror.

Matt put one foot up onto the bottom rail of the fence and turned to face David. "Mind telling me what you call this next part?" he asked. "The one you'd rather Sara show me than you tell me?" A grateful smile played at the corners of his mouth. This wasn't a consultation like any he'd ever experienced; frankly, it was maddeningly indirect. And yet, he knew in this moment that he'd come to the right place for help.

"The first capability we teach in our Engagement Equation is called 'challenge,'" David answered. "But far more important than what we call it is what it means, and for that, you're going to need to let Sara be your guide.

"Sara," he called, "Can you spare a few minutes with my friend Matt?"

"Just a second," she said, backing a few feet away from the horse. The mustang nickered, and then Sara turned from it and walked over to the fence where David and Matt were standing.

"It's nice to see you again, Sara," Matt said, extending his hand to the young cowgirl. He meant these words, his sincere face and kind eyes underscoring his greeting.

"It's nice to see you again, too, sir," Sara replied, shaking his hand firmly, her bearing proud and erect.

The guard remains at station, Matt thought, *but she's hoping for some company. Company she can trust.* Matt vowed to pass whatever tests Sara would throw at him.

"Sara's been learning and teaching horse training since she got here," David continued. "She's only been with us a year, Matt, but she has a gift with our wildest horses. They trust her," he continued, "and the trust of an unbroken horse is hard to earn."

A blush and small proud smile slipped past Sara's defenses. She gave her mentor a quick, appreciative glance, which he caught and then immediately released. In the half-second of exchange between them, Matt observed, David had given Sara the faintest nod of his head, the sparest smile imaginable, and an extraordinarily powerful acknowledgment. And just as quickly, he'd let her go—let her glance away and have her space.

"I teach my students how to treat a horse physically," David added, turning to Matt, "what gestures to use, how to approach the horse, read the horse's gestures, and how and when to back off. There's no mumbo jumbo here, either, just like there isn't with people. The difference with horses is that instead of closing the say-do gap, you have to close the gesture-do gap. It's still about your messages—in the horse's case, your bodily gestures—and how they need to match your intended actions. Make your gestures and your actions match in horse terms, and you'll gain the horse's trust."

"I trust them," Sara interjected, an edge of challenge in her voice. She glanced at David and then turned to Matt, squaring her body toward him. Matt suppressed the humorous image Sara's dress and pose had produced unbidden in his mind's eye of an Old West gunfighter. Life had brought this girl more than her share of adversaries.

"You can't work with horses like this if you don't trust them," Sara then declared, throwing down her gauntlet. "If you can't understand them or appreciate what it might be like to be them, these horses'll never let you in." Her remark was, indeed, a challenge. She continued to look at Matt, expecting a response.

David's face was relaxed, his eyes radiant. He gazed back and forth from Sara to Matt with a look of complete satisfaction. This was going exceedingly well and, if not according to plan precisely, certainly according to hope.

Matt looked at Sara for a moment longer and then nodded. "You know, Sara," he began, "you've just said something to me that I needed to hear."

Sara blinked. It wasn't the response she was expecting, and she needed to absorb this. It wasn't the response that would have disappointed her.

"Maybe David told you I'm having some problems in my company."

"You were saying something about that yesterday," Sara interjected. Matt noticed that she had stepped out of her gunfighter stance. They were just talking now.

"Well, I said yesterday that I'm not sure if my staff understands what I've been trying to communicate to them. David and I talked about this later, and he said the rock climb was not so much about communication as it was about trust. Do my staff members trust me and the things I'm trying to tell them?"

"I was introducing Matt to the trust part of our equation, Sara," David added, "and I told him that today we'd start in on the three capabilities. I'd like you to start him off with the first one."

Sara nodded that she understood the assignment.

"By the way, have you decided on a name, Sara?" David asked. Matt was confused, but Sara's face brightened.

"Sara is working with our newest equestrian recruit," David explained. "I started with him. In fact, I was working with him when you called me last week."

"His name's Arrow," Sara replied, "but I'd rather say that I finally learned his name. It doesn't seem right to say that I decided what it is."

"Why don't you tell us how you learned your horse's name," David suggested.

"Pretty simple, actually," Sara answered. "When he runs, he looks like he's flying, except not the way a bird flies. Arrow's flight is straight, fleet, and fast." She then smiled with satisfaction. What more was there to say?

"Just like an arrow," Matt deadpanned, enjoying playing the role of the straight man.

"Very quick," Sara allowed, enjoying the moment of lightness.

"Always said you were quick, my boy," David added, chuckling. "I need to check in with our head wrangler for a few minutes, Matt. Sara, could you spend a little more time with Matt right now and tell him about the first capability?"

"Happy to," she replied, looking as if she was glad to comply. "Just give me a second. Arrow's done for the day."

David left Matt by the corral fence and headed into one of the adjacent stables. Sara returned to Arrow; slowed her long, easy stride as she approached the horse; and then gently took his reins. Arrow gave a small snort and shook his head, as though to test the air and their bond, and then pressed his nose into Sara's shoulder. The ritual complete, Sara began leading Arrow from the corral back to the large, fenced field that was his current home.

Matt watched the horse and young woman as they walked away; he was mesmerized by the good chemistry between them that allowed them to move so smoothly and easily beside each other. He hadn't missed Sara's point in the least. *You can't work with a young woman like me if you can't understand me or appreciate what it might be like to be me. I'll never let you in,* Matt thought. *I came for one teacher and got two!*

———✦———

"What has David told you about the first capability we teach?" Sara asked. She had guided them to a latticed wooden double swing in the center of a small gazebo, canopied under the needles of a grove of tall Colorado pine that stood adjacent to the ranch's stables. Lemonades in hand, a ring-bound journal on the bench beside Sara, they sat on facing swings connected by the common running boards under their feet. This was a chance for them to talk at greater leisure and, Matt hoped, more deeply.

"Well," Matt began, searching for words to express what David had just told him. "He said you call the first capability 'challenge.' And he said—my words here—that you learn how to harness the raw potential in your people so that you get big results from them." He paused to read the expression on Sara's face. She nodded once, emphatically.

"And David said that it begins with trust. Leaders must close the say-do gap by doing what they say."

Sara simply nodded again. It was the student's turn to show what he knew, not the teacher's to offer instruction.

"So, did David say what the challenge capability is all about?"

"He just said that you'd explain that part to me," Matt answered.

Sara smiled. "Right." Now she knew where to begin. She opened her journal and flipped to a well-worn page.

"A leader must have a clear vision," she began, glancing up from her notes. "If you don't have a clear vision, you're not a leader."

Matt nodded.

"There are two parts to that," Sara added, the warning in her voice suggesting she wasn't sure Matt had stayed with her. "You have a vision," she enumerated, one finger raised, "and it's clear," she concluded, second finger joining the first.

Matt nodded again. He was with her.

Satisfied, Sara continued. "Around here, we call the leader's vision the great purpose. It all starts with great purpose—the leader must have an answer to the question, Why are we doing this? In other words, what's the great purpose behind this effort?"

"David and the leadership team told me about this. 'Every Child a Hope, Every Child a Home' is the great purpose of this ranch."

"That's right," Sara affirmed. "And we all live under that great purpose. To live at High Summit Ranch is to discipline yourself to make everything you do line up with 'Every Child a Hope, Every Child a Home.' But each of us is also a leader in smaller ways, so we each can establish goals that contribute to the ranch's overall vision.

"One of the newer goals, which I helped come up with, is to make wild mustangs as famous as whales." Sara paused, a trace of wariness visible around her eyes. She had stopped referring to her notes in her journal.

Matt nodded again. He was following her words closely. The leader knows the great purpose and sets goals that serve that purpose.

"We've had the goal of getting mustangs adopted for years, but my new goal is to get more people to know about them so more people will adopt them. Do you know the history of the western wild mustang?" Sara asked, laying her now-closed journal back onto the bench beside her.

"No, nothing at all, actually," Matt answered.

Sara explained to Matt that the mustang originated in North America and only disappeared from the continent within the past eight thousand years. The Spanish reintroduced mustangs to America, she explained, and the Indians soon adopted them fully into their lives. Over time, enough horses escaped from both the Spanish and the Indians to form wild herds throughout the West.

"In fact," Sara said, her voice taking on an edge of extra excitement, "they weren't called mustangs until they ran away. *Mesteños* means 'strayed' in Spanish. There's something about these horses that makes 'em want to run away." Sara's eyes were penetrating as she said these words.

Matt maintained eye contact with his new teacher and nodded his comprehension. She'd gotten an important point through to him. Mustangs needed room. Mustangs needed safety. She needed it, too.

Sara continued her story, telling Matt what happened over time to the great horses. The mustangs had no real predators, and their numbers grew, "which threatened the people who wanted to develop the land. That's why no one will recognize the mustang as original to this place," she explained. "If mustangs are original, they're protected, like the California condor. But the government calls them 'feral,' which means they can be slaughtered by the thousands. The stories are awful!"

Matt could see how the "strayed" had become so vulnerable. His heart was full with the story Sara was telling him about the mustangs and the story she was also telling him about herself.

"So, finally," Sara concluded, "the government stepped in and started an adoption program to place wild mustangs into good homes. But they don't come *close* to placing the number of mustangs needed. That's where my team and I come in."

"Getting the word out so more mustangs can be adopted," Matt filled in, moved and amazed by what he was hearing. This girl was throwing her whole heart into getting horses adopted, yet she was the one who needed the family.

"Exactly. Given our goal to make wild mustangs famous, several of us have started goal achievement teams to contribute to the overall success."

"Goal achievement teams," Matt repeated. "These are your work groups?"

"Sorry. It's all coming out in a jumble," Sara apologized. "Every kid gets to be a leader here. Every kid is helped to set a goal. And what's a leader with a goal if you don't have a team?" Sara asked this question with a look of seasoned incredulity. *Wasn't all of this obvious?*

"A leader needs people to help her, right?" Sara concluded, turning the corner to the question at hand. "So, what we're taught here is how to translate our goal into the Engagement Equation, and how to do this in a way that gets the right people onto the team so we can be successful.

"And that's what challenge is all about," she answered, taking a big breath.

Matt asked Sara to tell him more about this first capability, and she explained that challenge referred to everything involved in preparing a plan of action. The leader lays out the challenge to the team. She told him that there are three points to this capability. "Plans," she told him, holding up her index finger; "strengths," second finger; "roles," third finger.

"The leader issues a clear challenge," she summarized. "Here's the goal and plan. These are the talents and strengths needed. And here's who's going to do what, by when, and so forth. Clear?"

Matt was speechless, not because he had never heard of this kind of rigor but because a sixteen-year-old troubled girl was lecturing him on it.

"And we spend most of our time on the strengths and roles part. What are you good at? Where will you do the most good?

"Your mouth is hanging open," Sara said, giggling.

"That's because what you just told me is like what they tried to teach me in graduate school," Matt answered, closing his mouth.

Sara's face broke into her biggest smile yet, a teenager's smile this time, happy, carefree, and animated by the wonder of getting to do something so important. She seemed especially glad that Matt could respect her sincere efforts to do something important and treat her like a grown-up.

Matt returned Sara's smile, caught her eye for a second, and then settled back into the swing, turning his gaze toward the majestic peaks to the west, nothing else on his mind but the young woman before him. He was giving her space, taking a lesson from David, letting her make her own choices.

Matt thought again about Molly. In the beginning, she'd closed a string of new sales. She'd been relentless in pursuing new prospects, yet all the while she was so winsome, thoughtful, and charming that no one ever minded her hounding.

Matt had promoted Molly to account management. Clients had enjoyed her as a sales rep, so they'd asked for her to stay on their accounts. Molly had expressed uncertainty about the move, but Matt had explained that providing ongoing service to customers that you've already won was a whole lot easier than trying to win new customers. Besides, he'd just lost an account manager, and she had been specifically requested.

He knew Molly would need to learn some new skills to excel in management the way she had in sales, but growth is always a learning process. He'd felt sure, after all, that the stability of account management would be preferable to Molly over the constant uncertainty of new sales.

Matt's sense of incompetence deepened as he thought about what he'd done. He'd had a superstar in sales. So he'd reassigned her. He'd thought of it as the normal career path. He believed he was helping her progress just as others had helped him—from sales to account management, account management to team leadership. Matt felt sick.

"I'm forming a new team, Matt," Sara said, her voice now hesitant. Absentmindedly, she reached down and retrieved her journal. She had Matt's attention. "I want to train Arrow to compete at the national level in barrel racing. We've never had a national speed-racing champion from mustang stock, and I thought of this as a way to get mustangs better known." Sara was talking fast now, her words less confident, her face a plea. The journal she held was clutched with white knuckles. The young woman had transformed back into a child right before Matt's eyes. "David says he's special, very special. He says he's never seen a horse with such build and spirit. I wanna race him, Matt!" Sara concluded, her declaration as much an appeal as a statement. "Will you join my new team?"

There it was. Matt had wondered what had turned this confident young woman into a pleading girl; she wanted him to help her. And just how was he in a position to help her? He couldn't help himself.

"I don't know anything about horses," Matt answered, his own voice betraying the despair he was feeling.

"I know about horses," Sara answered, "and so do our head wrangler and David. You'll be good at stuff we're not good at."

"I live in New York," Matt felt he had to point out.

"Can't you help from New York?" she asked, her voice smaller still. "What are you good at?" she added, finally. It was the question they were drilled to ask. *What am I good at? What are you good at?* But the tone in which she asked it was edged with disappointment; she was now wondering whether Matt was going to be good for anything, good for her. She was wondering, in truth, whether she could be helped at all.

Matt leaned forward, put his elbows onto his knees, and his head into his hands. He wasn't good at *this*; that much was certain. His wife would totally agree. A human being was sitting right in front of him, needing more from him than she was getting, asking for more. Just like Alice was asking. Just like his staff. Just like his executive team at Lumina.

Matt's head jerked straight back up, his reanimation so sudden that Sara jumped. Seeing Matt's expression of wonder, Sara laughed outright. She couldn't help herself; Matt looked like he had an idea, and she was in great need of one.

"Advertising!" Matt exclaimed. "It's what I do!"

"Are you good at it?" Sara asked, then giggling at the way her question came out. She meant to ask him if this was his strength, not whether he was competent at his job.

Matt laughed along with her, but not as merrily. "Good at advertising, yes. Great at it, as a matter of fact. I was one of the best," he threw in, shaking his head ruefully. "Sara, I'm great at advertising and marketing, which is why I was promoted to head up my company's New Strategies and Clients Division. But you need to know that I'm pretty close to being a total failure in the 'heading up' business."

"That's why you're here?" Sara asked, her gaze level, her footing resecured.

"That's why I'm here."

"Good," she exclaimed brightly, opening up her journal and making a notation. "So you help me with advertising, and I'll help you with heading up." Sara then smiled. He could help her. She could help him. How great was that?

"What's in the journal, by the way?" Matt asked. Sara glanced up with a startled expression. "I don't mean to be personal," Matt quickly added, a small blush creeping up his cheek. "I saw you write something down a second ago."

Sara giggled. "There's nothing personal here," she said. "I thought David would have already told you about our journals. I'm surprised he didn't. Here," she added, handing her journal to Matt. The cover read

Goal Achievement Journal
Preparation, Implementation, Evaluation

BY SARA JARREL

"Look here," Sara added, reaching across Matt's grip on the journal to turn to a page filled with her careful hand lettering. "This covers what we just discussed," she added.

Matt quickly scanned the page she had chosen for him. He turned the page and saw that Sara's journal was a detailed workbook, with step-by-step guidance in clarifying vision and mission, in making goals, in planning, in project implementation and management, and in evaluation. Seeing this, he got a good idea of David's plans for his next few days. And he saw that Sara had filled in many of the worksheets that were provided in the journal.

$$T \times 3C = E$$
Engagement Equation

T (closing "the say-do gap")

Trust (the leader's credibility)

3C (closing "the paycheck-purpose gap")

Challenge (preparation stage)

Plans, strengths, roles

Learn to <u>receive</u>

"Closing 'the paycheck-purpose gap'?" Matt then asked. "What's that?"

"That will make sense later," Sara replied. "You handle the three *C*s right—the preparation stage, the implementation stage, and then the evaluation stage, and it changes the way people feel about doing their jobs. David says that lots of people feel that their work is pretty meaningless—that it's just a paycheck."

"Did I hear my name?" David was strolling toward his younger charges, a big smile on his face.

"Actually, it was just getting good, David," Matt said, a little irritated, truth be told, by the interruption of his looking at Sara's journal.

"Did you get him?" David asked Sara.

"Got 'im!" She answered, reaching over to retrieve her journal from her newest teammate. "He's gonna join my new goal achievement team. And if he wants, I'm gonna join his, once he tells me what it is." She was looking quite herself again.

"This was a recruitment meeting!" Matt exclaimed, a look of amazement on his face as he glanced back and forth at the satisfied smiles of his new and old friends.

———

"And do you mind also telling me about Sara, David?" Matt asked. "What got her here? What's driving her so hard? Why is she so afraid?" Dinner was long over, and the evening was nearly spent. The two of them had spoken together for a while in David's office before departing for a final outdoor activity before bedtime. Small solar-charged pathway lights lined both sides of the trail, their soft blue radiance guiding them up a gentle incline into the foothills just above the ranch house.

Matt's day had been filled with introductions to Sara's new team as well as a formal meeting of her goal achievement team that included David; the ranch's head wrangler, Stu; several other students Matt met for the first time; and Tyler, the young boy who'd made his first rock-face descent the day before. During Sara's team meeting, David provided a review of the elements of the second capability, called "charge," and Matt took pleasure in having already peeked ahead at this capability in Sara's journal.

During the balance of the day, Tyler had gravitated to Matt; he was always in the chair next to him or just behind his elbow whenever they moved from site to site. At supper, Matt had called Tyler over to him and had pulled up a chair for the boy next to him. Throughout the meal, the little fourth grader had eyes for no one other than his big new friend. After dinner, David had spoken sternly to Matt. "I love the interest you're taking in the boy," he'd said as they sat together in his office, "but if you're going to start a relationship with Tyler, be prepared to stay in a relationship with him. Write him notes, call him, send him little gifts sometimes. Tyler needs people who stay in touch."

Continuing up the solar-lighted pathway, David spoke of Sara. "In her case, Matt," he said, "I'd rather she tell you her story. Let her bring you into her life the way she prefers. She'll trust you more that way."

Matt accepted—indeed, saw great wisdom in—David's reluctance to talk about Sara's past. They then walked easily beside each other, Matt filling David in on what he had learned about the capability called challenge.

"When we work with the horses here, Matt, and with the kids, we receive them as they are. We love them and we appreciate them. That's our starting point." David pulled the two of them to a halt just shy of a fire circle that was surrounded by several dozen youths and staff from the ranch.

"You don't start with what's wrong with these kids," Matt remarked, remembering David's comments earlier; *could it have been only this morning?*

"When a leader prepares to get something done, he starts by asking people to contribute what strengths and assets they have to accomplish the plan. He fits the strengths together by assigning people to roles in which they can succeed. What we must learn is how to be a receiver. We must always be in a posture of receiving, of appreciating, of loving; we must do that if we want the people who help us to eventually take the risk of bringing their whole selves to the effort."

"I think it must be very affirming to these youths to have people help them achieve their goals. It must really build up their feeling of self-worth," Matt offered.

"Let you in on a secret, Matt," David replied. "These kids don't gain a sense of worth by accomplishing goals. A sense of capability, yes, but not of worth."

Matt waited for David to make sense of this curious comment.

"Paradoxically, they gain a sense of their worth by serving on the teams of their classmates. When they realize that they're important to someone else, when they serve someone else's goals and dreams, that's when the really good stuff happens. Might work that way for you, too, my friend," David added. "C'mon. They're waiting for us."

Matt followed David into the fire circle, his mind scrambling to connect what he just heard with his leadership crisis in New York. How often did he seek out Randy's expertise when he was plagued by a problem in his division? How often did he invite any of his sales leaders to solve the leadership and performance problems he was suffering? It had not occurred to him to do this. He was the leader after all. Wasn't he the one who was supposed to give the answers? But David had just told him that the really good things start to happen when leaders become receivers.

What could his team have told him if he'd been listening? What did Randy already know about what had gone wrong? What did Molly know? If he had pulled them in, how might they have guided his decisions to better outcomes?

The star-studded night lay so closely across the canopy of sky over their heads that Matt felt he could reach up and run his fingers through its dazzling tresses.

"A passage from the Psalms," was all the preamble David offered. "Please look up," he added, clearing his throat and waiting for all sounds of feet and hushed whispers to still. Crackling snaps and spits of hungry fire blended in with the dry chirp of a thousand crickets, together producing a ground cover of sound that perfectly suited the sky cover of blazing stars.

"As far as the heavens are above the earth," David then recited, his voice clear and resonant, "so great is God's love for us."

Matt waited for his mentor to continue and then realized that David was finished. The bright percussive crackle of the fire joined by the chorusing crickets reclaimed the nighttime soundscape. Each of the men and women in the circle was left to his or her own thoughts, tucked comfortingly within the cover of sound that enveloped them.

As far as the heavens are above the earth. Matt considered the words he had just heard and tried to fathom the scale of them. *So great is God's love for us.* He shook his head. What he couldn't fathom, more than the vastness of the universe that stretched above him, was the possibility that he might be loved this much, that anyone—God especially—would ever want to. Matt's gaze turned downward into the crackling fire, his thoughts gone deeply private.

One by one the students and staff drifted away from the circle, returning down the path to their beds. David held his place, watching until only Matt remained, transfixed, before the fire. David considered his friend's situation for a few moments; he wished he could retreat and give Matt the deep privacy he was sure he needed right now. But there were overriding considerations—his friend was a rather helpless city boy, and mountain lions liked to roam the area.

"Ready to go, my friend?" David finally asked, his voice quiet and deep.

"Go where?" Matt answered, looking up at his mentor.

David smiled his understanding back at Matt. It was an excellent question, one he had asked himself on more than one important occasion.

"For now, to bed," he answered, his smile unwavering. "As for tomorrow, Matt, God only knows."

DIRECTING
THE
CHARGE

I've only told you part of the story, David." Matt was sitting in his mentor's apartment suite—a bedroom, bath, and sitting room David occupied within the larger sprawling ranch house—on the large leather couch, his pajama-clad friend across from him in the massive armchair.

When Matt knocked on David's door, it had opened almost immediately, his friend looking totally awake, almost expectant. Matt had lain in bed for the greater part of an hour—another too-early wake-up facilitated by his New York body clock—and finally arose with resolve to pad his way down the hall to the door he'd seen David enter the night before. He'd felt stupid doing this, stupid and weak, but he did it anyway. It was his night, he figured, his turn to wake up the old man. Every hour he spent on this ranch made him feel more like one of the youths and less like one of the grown-ups.

"My problems aren't just at work." Matt made this comment with the grim resolve of a penitent determined to tell his confessor the rest of the story.

David's face was as pleasant and relaxed as could be; he might have been running a currycomb across the withers of his favorite horse or gazing into the mountain-peaked sunset after a well-spent day. Nothing could have possibly surprised him less than Matt's revelation that he might have an extra problem or two.

"My marriage," Matt started, and then as suddenly stopped, his voice washed away in a dam break of emotion he'd been holding back for a long time. His face was in his hands, the restraints of long training insufficient to hold back his tears. *It really is my night*, Matt thought, amazed at what had just leapt, unforeseen, from within him. The sorrow would not be denied, and he watched his own loss of control with true amazement.

David waited, and Matt slowly regained his breath.

"Alice and I were married nineteen years ago," Matt began, directing his comments toward his hands, which he now had clasped on his lap. "We'd dated pretty much straight through graduate school and really loved each other."

David took a deep breath and let it out. A marriage that started out with great love always had enormous hope, he'd come to learn, however damaged the marriage had since become.

"You introduced me to Alice, Matt," David interjected. The uncertain look on Matt's face revealed that he'd forgotten this fact. "I spoke with her briefly at your graduation and sensed the truth of what you just said; she really loved you."

"She did," Matt replied. "And I her. But then came the work—hours and hours and years and years of work. She pursued law while I pursued advertising. And it really seemed okay. It was exciting and we loved each other." Matt paused to consider which direction to take next.

"Alice just turned forty-four," he added, looking up imploringly. "David, we've tried to have a baby for five years. We didn't think we wanted children. Alice didn't," he added. "Well, I didn't either. And then, well . . ." Matt paused again. "We changed our minds."

David continued to wait, knowing there was more.

"There's no explanation, David. We saw everybody, tried everything, and there's no explanation." Matt's distress was rising visibly; he was twisting his hands, shaking his head back and forth. David waited.

"We wanted a baby so badly," Matt continued, his voice louder. "We really wanted a baby, wanted one with all our hearts, and we can't forgive ourselves."

David sat forward, every fiber of his being on full alert. Matt wrung his hands, rubbing them together as though he were washing them under a stream of water. And then he stopped; his eyes rose to meet David's.

"Alice was pregnant," he said simply. "She was twenty-two, in her first year of law school. I was twenty-five, fresh into business school. We hadn't dated long, and it was the wrong time for Alice to be pregnant. She'd have needed to drop her program," he added, his face imploring.

"What were we thinking?" Matt then added, barely getting these final, desperate words out, his face twisted in perfect torment. "Oh, my God," he whispered, his hands covering his head.

David was out of his seat and beside Matt in a stroke, his arm around his friend as Matt tried to steady his breath. Long minutes passed with David simply repeating, "I'm sorry, Matt."

"It would have been a boy," Matt added, the words so small, the pain of them so enormous.

"You're living with regrets, Matt," David finally said, pulling back enough from his friend to look him in the eyes. His words were firm, but his gaze could not have been kinder or his face softer. "The decision seemed right when you made it. You drew from what you knew and made a decision that seemed to you at the time to be the best."

Matt nodded his acknowledgment of the truth of these words.

"Now you look back and have terrible regrets. Time, life, and learning have changed how you think and feel about what you did."

Matt nodded again. That's what had happened. They had been in a nightmare of turmoil when Alice discovered she was pregnant and after days of shock and confusion had done what seemed sensible. Wherever they turned for guidance, their decision was judged sensible. Now they wanted nothing more than to push away the memory of what they'd done. And in the process, they were pushing each other away.

"You're trying to forgive yourselves, and you don't know how," David continued, responding to his younger friend's words. "And it's tearing the two of you apart."

Listening to these words, Matt knew that he still loved Alice. He loved her fiercely, as a matter of fact. And this was precisely what he couldn't bear. What he wanted to push away was the great pain he felt whenever he looked at her, whenever he remembered what they'd done.

"Matt," David said, his voice again very firm. He wanted Matt's attention. "Every human being has terrible regrets. We do things we can't forgive ourselves for, and eventually our heart breaks. It does," he added, "if there's hope for us. Listen to me."

David had Matt's full attention. The firmness of his voice, the toughness of his words riveted the younger man. Matt might have been an abandoned boy in a burning house receiving stern shouts of instruction from a smoke-blackened rescuer. The words he was hearing were lifelines. Their toughness made them all the better for the job. He was listening.

"Around here, we call this the 'stumble.' You and Alice stumbled, the price of your stumble is incalculable, and you haven't been able to pay the bill." Matt's eyes didn't waver from David's. "You'll never be able to pay it, Matt. You need to know this. No heroics and no amount of effort can change this fact. You can't fix what you did. Welcome to the human race, my friend," David added, everything about his bearing and face and voice having shifted into perfect kindness.

Matt just stared at his mentor. In some fashion, he already knew this. He'd screwed up big time. Now he couldn't bear it, and there wasn't a thing he could do about it.

"You're wondering if I have any good news for you," David said.

"Well, yes and no," Matt replied. "I needed to hear what you just said, even though I already knew it. It's a good thing to learn that the reason you're stuck is that you're stuck. Rather than that you aren't trying hard enough, I mean. I've tried everything I know, David."

"Yes, you have," David said. "So the real question is, do you have to stay stuck?"

Matt shrugged. Wasn't the answer obvious?

"The answer's no. You don't have to stay stuck. You can't fix what you did, but what you did can be fixed.

"And for now, would you just take my word for it? Let me show you some things. I promise you we'll talk this through, but I believe my words will make more sense if I can show you first."

Matt was deep in thought. He already knew David's mode of operation, so no surprise here. And this was only his third day, barely his third day, as a matter of fact. The windows in David's suite had turned from black to early-morning pale. David had told him that there was a way out and that he'd show him what it was. So, yeah, he was good to go with David's plan. What did he have to lose that wasn't already lost?

Matt nodded, offering his mentor a tight-lipped smile of agreement and thanks.

"Coffee?" David inquired.

"Sure," Matt replied, unable to mask a small grimace at the thought.

———◆◆———

"My name's Sara."

"Hi, Sara!" a chorus of young voices responded, along with those of John, Stu, David, Teddy, and several other ranch staff. Matt hadn't been quick enough on the draw to chime in. Everyone else in the ranch's conference room already knew the drill and responded instantly and in unison to Sara's declaration.

"I'll be sixteen years old on Sunday." She glanced nervously over to the side where Matt was seated, and then she continued, "But more importantly, today is my four hundredth day of being clean."

Cheers and applause erupted from the room. Sara blushed, smiled, and glanced again in Matt's direction.

At breakfast, David had asked Matt to join their "Friday start," as he called it. "It's part of our weekly orientation for the newest arrivals," he had said. "It runs every Friday morning throughout their first six months on the ranch."

Matt was ecstatic. Since arriving on Wednesday, he had wanted more formal input, a more traditional consultancy, truth be told. David was telling him to show up at an orientation. *No saddle sores* was also what he was thinking.

"Sara asked me last night if you would be coming, Matt," David had added, "and when I said I'd bring you, she volunteered to do the lead for the meeting." David's expression conveyed some great significance to what he was telling Matt though Matt wasn't sure what the significance was. Perhaps Sara wanted to show him that she knew how to lead, which she had said she was going to do, so that made sense enough.

"You don't know what a lead is, do you?" David asked, reading Matt's face easily.

"Um, I guess not," Matt decided to say. He'd thought of taking a shot at it—it was sure to have something to do with leadership—and then thought better of it. "Does it involve horses?" he decided to ask, just to be sure.

David just grinned at Matt's naïveté, thumping Matt once on the back.

"What this means, Matt," David continued, his face quickly losing its grin, "is that Sara has decided to let you in. She wants to do the lead because she wants you to hear it."

After Matt took his seat, Tyler scooted over several chairs to join him. Matt now realized just how recent the little boy's arrival had been.

"Mom died when I was nine," Sara was continuing, "and my father arranged for me to live with his sister. He said he needed some time. He said he'd come for me." Sara paused, blinked twice, and then continued. "I haven't seen my dad or heard from him in over six years. I needed my dad," Sara said, now looking directly at Matt, "but my dad decided that his problems were more important than mine."

Sara turned back to the roomful of youths, and Matt's heart was broken. Her last statement was not made challengingly. Her face held no accusation. She wasn't throwing down a gauntlet—"Don't be like my dad." She had shared her feelings with him. She had told him an intimate truth about herself because she wanted him to know.

Tyler was leaning against Matt's arm now; he had slid farther over during Sara's last remarks about her father.

"I started smoking when I was twelve and turned to marijuana almost immediately and then to crack." Sara's voice had become much quieter. She wasn't looking at anyone now. Her gaze was fixed on the floor in front of her feet.

"My aunt kicked me out just before I turned fourteen. I looked and acted older than I was, and I earned my drug money with sex." A quick glance toward Matt, her breath frozen, stole past Sara's resolve. Matt missed it as his own eyes were fixed on the floor, brimming with tears. Sara saw the tears and began to breathe again.

"I got arrested a little over a year ago," she continued. "They figured out my age, put me in detox, and then sent me here."

Sara looked up at the mostly ten- through fourteen-year-olds sitting in front of her. She knew their stories weren't far off from hers, different in the details but filled with their own horrors. She smiled, her face suddenly flush with kindness and understanding.

"Each morning I thank God that I'm alive and clean. I thank God for David Butler," she added, looking over to the man who kept his promises. David did not deflect the acknowledgment, returning her gaze evenly. "I thank God for this place, and every day I offer myself to God. He can have me," Sara then stated, her face now hard with a resolve born of truth. "He uses me better than anyone else ever did.

"I do this every day," Sara repeated. "One day at a time," she said finally, and then sat down.

The youths and adults applauded. "That was great, Sara," "Love you, Sara," and other affirming remarks chorused from the assembly.

"Thank you, Sara," Teddy chimed in, rising to take her place at the front of the assembly. *Horse and Saddle Monthly* had nothing to offer the Harvard boy in the haberdashery department, nor could John Wayne or Clint Eastwood have coached him further in his affectation of a casual, cowboy slouch. A click of the micro-infrared remote concealed in his palm brought a PowerPoint screen to life, which instantly assured the assembly that this cowboy was of the unthreatening urban variety. The screen had the formula "$T \times 3C = E$" across the top in large print; the rest of the page was blank.

"John has debriefed each of you on the rock climb from Wednesday," Teddy said, instantly down to business. He clicked the mouse, first adding a section on the chart addressing trust, and with another click the C capability called challenge.

$$T \times 3C = E$$
Engagement Equation
T (closing "the say-do gap")

Trust (the leader's credibility)

$3C$ (closing "the paycheck-purpose gap")

　Challenge (preparation stage)

　　Plans, strengths, roles

　　Learn to <u>receive</u>

"Challenge," Teddy launched in, "is what we do first in our Engagement Equation. It's the preparation stage for our projects. What's your plan? Is it clear? What strengths do you have in the mix of the team? How are you going to arrange yourselves to let people be best at what they're best at and to achieve the goals you've set? The best thing you learned from the climb, please?" Teddy then asked.

"You might not know what you're good at," a young girl offered from the front. Matt had seen her at the rock climb but didn't remember her name.

"Great, Mary. What made you realize this?" Teddy probed.

"Well, Tyler didn't think he'd be good at rappelling," she began. Tyler stirred, bracing himself for the likely insult. "But he looked fantastic coming down the climb, like he was a master." Tyler glanced up, his face radiant as he caught the smile Mary flashed at him and returned it with interest.

"So we might not know what our strengths are, but others might know," Teddy offered, "and that's why we must learn to receive if we're going to master this capability. We receive new information about ourselves from others, and we also receive the strengths of others who want to help us achieve our goal. Can you receive if you aren't thankful?" Teddy then asked.

"Well," Mary continued, "if you aren't thankful, you won't know that what you have is good. You won't keep it, or you'll waste it or throw it away."

"Fabulous, Mary!" Teddy enthused. "We get good stuff all the time, but if we have no appreciation inside of us, all the good stuff will just slip right through our fingers while we whine about how nothing good ever comes to us." Teddy spoke the last part of this sentence with a huge, comical frown, his voice very nasal, his mouth twisted down at both corners like Eeyore's.

"Got that?" Teddy asked loudly, his own voice restored. Vigorous nods and big smiles were offered in reply.

"That's the review from last Friday. The second capability," Teddy continued, pulling his infrared trigger, "moves us from the challenge to the charge, from the preparation stage to the implementation stage.

"In the implementation stage we expect to make mistakes. It's normal. Now that we're doing the stuff we planned to do, we're going to have to deal with constant surprises. The first word here is 'innovate.' What does that word mean?" Teddy asked.

$$T \times 3C = E$$
Engagement Equation

T (closing "the say-do gap")

Trust (the leader's credibility)

3C (closing "the paycheck-purpose gap")

Challenge (preparation stage)

Plans, strengths, roles

Learn to <u>receive</u>

Charge (implementation stage)

Innovate, scan, adjust

Learn to <u>release</u>

The newest residents of the camp looked stumped, and the older members held their tongues.

"It means 'try new stuff,'" Teddy answered. "When we innovate, we're doing things in ways never tried before. And if something's never been tried before, how's it going to turn out?"

"Who knows?" Tyler ventured, glancing nervously up at Matt, who gave him a vigorous thumbs-up for the perfect answer.

"Exactly. It's never been tried, so who knows if it'll work? It might be fantastic, so we give it a go. Or it might flop totally. We might fall on our nose." The PowerPoint clicked, Teddy pausing to allow the youths to read the words he'd put on the screen.

Innovate! Try the untried. Do the thing that "can't be done."
The worst that'll happen is you'll stumble and fall. While
you're down there, why don't you roll over onto your back
and look up at the mind-boggling stars for a minute. Then
get back up!

MIKE WILSON
Graduation Address 2006, High Summit Ranch

"What's the second word under 'charge'?" Teddy pressed on.

"Scan," several youths said in unison.

"Meaning?"

"Look around," Mary answered.

"Right! So you're either on the ground already, or you're
headed there," Teddy continued. "Have a look around. Give it a
360. What can you learn? When we're implementing our plans,
friends, our focus is not on having to be right. Our focus is on
constant learning. Innovate, scan, and the third word is?"

"Adjust," called out the children.

"Which means, quite simply, let it go. You were trying it
one way, now try it another. Learn to release your tight grip.
Adjust. The point of the implementation stage is to always
keep going, keep learning, keep growing. Make sense?"

Some of the children nodded their heads; Teddy's words
were a welcome relief to their scrappy entrepreneurial spirits.
Others sat still; too many punishments—self-inflicted and
otherwise—had already come to them for things they hadn't
gotten right for them to just take Teddy at his word that failing was okay.

"Stand up for me, Tyler," Teddy said. Tyler stood, looking
around for some clue as to what was about to happen. No one
had any more idea than he did. "Now I want you to run up to

me here in front when I say 'go.' Just as fast as you can, Tyler. Go!" he shouted, and Tyler ran, jackrabbit-like, around several desks and up to where Teddy was standing. Tyler glanced back at Matt, a big smile on his face. He'd made the dash in a flash!

"Were there marks on the floor to tell you where to put your feet, Tyler?" Teddy asked.

"No!" Tyler snorted.

"Did you know ahead of time exactly where each foot was going to go?" Teddy pressed.

"No!" Tyler was feeling more confident by the second.

"So you had no plan?" Teddy challenged playfully.

"To get up here," Tyler retorted.

"So you did have a plan, then," Teddy replied, "but you started moving without knowing everything that might go wrong. Mary might have stuck out her leg to trip you."

"I'd have jumped over it," Tyler laughed.

"Or tripped and fallen," Teddy offered.

"Yeah, or I'd have tripped and fallen."

"So why'd you start running if you didn't know everything that might happen?" Teddy asked.

"I wouldn't have gotten here if I hadn't," Tyler answered, once again glancing over at Matt. He got *two* vigorous thumbs-up for this answer.

"Good job, Tyler," Teddy said, patting the boy on the back. "One more question. Were your eyes open or closed while you ran up here?"

"Open!" Tyler nearly crowed. He'd been called to the front of the class. He'd gone. And he wasn't made fun of; on the contrary, he'd succeeded.

"Innovate, scan, adjust!" Teddy repeated. "It's the only way to get somewhere. You never ever forget where you're going.

But you know your plans will hit snags. It's always a risk to try to do something important, there's always a stumble, it's always about learning, and you keep your eyes open.

"Sara," Teddy continued. "It's time for the hands-on part of this lesson. The class is yours."

Sara was on her feet in an instant. "Bathrooms, a snack in the mess hall, and be at the corral in thirty minutes sharp. Don't be late!" she added sternly.

———•◦•———

"Who's Mike Wilson?" Matt asked Teddy. They were walking back across the same field Matt and David had crossed the previous day. The brilliant clarity of the midmorning sun made the snow-crusted peaks to the west almost pop out of the scene before them. The red stables and white-fenced corrals they were approaching, nestled gorgeously in the lap of these grand peaks, made the phrase "pretty as a postcard" seem ridiculously inadequate to describe the spectacular view.

"Mike Wilson's the son of a friend of Butler's. Late friend, I should say. David brought Mike here last year to teach us a model of leadership he learned from his late father, a former CEO named Robert Wilson. Robert called his model Serving Leadership, and Mike travels around the world coaching people on how to put the model into action."

"Is that what you teach here?" Matt asked.

"Ultimately, yes. But we've zeroed in on one part of Serving Leadership that Mike calls Build on Strength. Our whole three-capability strategy for goal achievement drills Mike's concept of building on strength down into its specifics. David thought this was the best place to start with the kids we get."

"Do you always mix classroom with hands-on learning?" Matt asked. They were rounding the gazebo where he and Sara had started to really talk. *Could it have been just yesterday?* Matt wondered. He could not comprehend how much was happening in such a short span of days. And already tomorrow—Saturday, a day before Sara's sixteenth birthday—was his date for return to New York. To Alice. To everything that was broken in his life. *Would his life always be so totally broken? Always feel so unfixable?*

"Always!" Teddy answered emphatically. Matt jerked his head in Teddy's direction, his jaw agape at the fact that Teddy had apparently read his mind.

"The classroom's good," Teddy continued, oblivious to Matt's shock. "But David's a big believer in hands-on. We don't engage these kids through theory. We engage them in real life, real work, real projects," Teddy added. "So, yeah, we always do both here.

"Here we are," Teddy added, his voice lowered to not disturb the group they had joined. Matt pulled himself the rest of the way out of his dark, private ruminations and took in the scene before him. They had walked up to the rear of the group of students, now reassembled along the fence around one of the riding corrals. Sara and David were inside the fence with Arrow, who was standing twenty paces behind them, his head turned in their direction to watch them. Sara was speaking.

"Before I go on," Sara said, turning to Matt and Teddy, "I want to catch our new friend up on what we've been doing." All eyes turned to the back of the group, and in an instant, Tyler slipped away from the side of the group where he'd been standing to come next to Matt, who, without looking down, laid a hand on his young friend's shoulder. He executed the gesture as naturally as possible, calling no special attention to it. They were buds, after all. Wasn't this place, right by his side, Tyler's place? What's there to comment on? Feeling Matt's hand on his shoulder, Tyler closed ranks the rest of the way with his big friend and turned to face Sara as though she were addressing him now, too.

David Butler's eyes moved from Matt's to Tyler's and back again to Matt's. He recognized the boy's bonding with the man and wondered about the man's bonding with the boy. These children's needs and the frequency with which adults let them down broke his heart. Their courage to keep reaching out in search of someone to return their love shamed him. Taking Tyler into his life—for a few days or for a lifetime—wouldn't solve Matt's problems, David knew. It wouldn't pay his debts, absolve his sins, or rebalance the scales of his life. One child never replaced another, David knew too well. An act of love, however excellent in its own right, never wiped out an act of harm. It didn't work that way.

"Matt joined my goal achievement team yesterday, but not everyone had a chance to meet him," Sara continued, "so let's welcome him!" The group applauded, and Matt blushed. He hadn't done anything worthy of applause and wondered if he could.

"Matt, I've pulled my team together several times over the past week—ever since I set my new goal to make Arrow into a top speed racer. We believe Arrow is going to be very fast. He's got the raw talent, the speed, and the heart that it takes."

"The idea came to Sara," David broke in, "while she was reading about a mustang named CJ who got real close to the top several years ago. As CJ gained visibility through his success in speed racing, families who were considering getting a horse thought about mustangs. Adoptions of mustangs went up over 25 percent while CJ was racing."

"You've had Arrow how long?" Matt asked. It wasn't really the question that was on his mind, but it seemed the politest way to get at it.

"Exactly!" Sara answered. She'd heard the real question. "It's sinking in that, under the best of circumstances, Arrow's not going to be ready to make any news for at least a year and a half. We won't throw a blanket onto his back, let alone a saddle, for another week or two. And getting me up there comes later, and teaching him how to run the track, later still." Her face wore discouragement.

"The goal is to get more people to adopt mustangs, but now that we've started fleshing out the plan to serve that goal, it feels like it's going to take practically forever to get there. And, of course, he might *never* get there."

"Which is why," Teddy jumped in, "Sara asked for a charge meeting. Sara's plan is to race Arrow. This serves our goal to make wild mustangs famous. And this serves our purpose of increasing their adoption."

The children and youths nodded their heads vigorously as Teddy repeated the things they knew. Matt's head shook in the opposite direction. He could hardly take in the sight—or the emotions—of a group of unadopted kids enthusiastically throwing themselves into the task of getting some horses adopted.

"So, back to our review from earlier," Teddy continued. "What's Sara's innovation?"

"Setting a new goal about horse racing to contribute to our goal of getting more adoptions," said a student whose name Matt didn't know.

"Good, Alycia," Teddy responded. "That's Sara's innovation. And what do we do after we innovate?" he reviewed.

"Scan," said Tyler. Matt squeezed his shoulder.

"We scan," Teddy repeated. "And why do we scan?" he asked.

"Stuff might go wrong," said Bobby.

"Or not as right as it could go," said Michelle.

"Either way," affirmed Teddy. "We scan, 'cause our results might not be coming in like we thought, or because we might be able to get even better results than we first thought. The point, remember, is to constantly learn and improve. Innovate, scan, adjust. Keep going! Keep growing! Remember?"

Heads nodded energetically.

"So, at our team meeting last night," Sara resumed, stepping back into the exercise, "we talked about how long my goal's going to take. I had thought at first that I'd be pulling down blue ribbons in a week or so." She made this comment with a self-effacing smile that invited easy laughter, and the children did laugh; it was good to know that they weren't the only ones whose hopes and dreams ran into snags. Even older, really amazing kids like Sara had disappointments.

"I now know that I've got years of work facing me, and no guarantee of reaching my goal of national renown. And the goal isn't even for its own sake," she reminded them. "The racing goal is for the purpose of serving the adoption goal. So we decided to bring this problem to everybody," Sara concluded.

"This is what charge is like, friends," Teddy added. "We lay out our plans in the preparation stage, and now that we've started to implement our plans, something always comes up that feels like a failure or a disappointment or an impossible problem. But it isn't!" he concluded emphatically. "It's just another step on the way to success."

Sara then walked slowly, gracefully, and purposefully out into the center of the corral and greeted Arrow with a hand on his nose. Arrow responded by nuzzling up against Sara. One could see the chemistry of trust flowing between them. Who could call this a failure? The children watched, and no one missed the point that great things had already happened, if not exactly the things Sara had first dreamed. She'd won the horse's trust. They'd forged a bond. What had been a snorting terror was now a horse named Arrow, and his warm, velvet-soft nose was nuzzled into Sara's neck, her arms looped easily around the mighty steed's head as she pulled her fingers through the long flowing hair of his beautiful mane. *Anybody want to call this a failure?*

Sara stepped back from Arrow, half-turning away from him but keeping an eye on him all the while. Her gesture conveyed the expectation that she would be followed. Arrow turned in her direction and took a step toward her. As though holding him by an invisible lead, Sara began walking very slowly toward the students, her back now fully to Arrow, her head turned to the side to tell her horse that she was leading, not leaving. Arrow followed his leader and came to a stop a few feet behind where Sara paused beside her mentor, David. Her hand was up, signaling the students to be quiet and still.

"We're making progress," she said simply. "But no amount of progress changes the fact that my real goal—increasing adoptions—won't be impacted by our training work for a very long time."

Matt was transfixed by what he was witnessing. Sara wasn't much more than a week into the implementation of a major plan, and she was already naming problems. She was telling her team what wasn't working. She was asking for their input.

When had he ever done this? "Why don't you ask them?" Deb had often suggested. Matt never paid attention to this suggestion, but he realized now that Deb had offered this thought many times. He would let a complaint slip: What was Molly thinking? Why has Randy slacked off? Can't design finish on time at least once? "Why don't you ask them?" Deb would suggest, as if it were that simple. Just ask them!

Sara wasn't giving up on her goal. She wasn't announcing a new goal to fudge the fact that an old one had gone belly up. Matt had done that on more than one occasion, he admitted. Okay, he'd done it embarrassingly often.

Sara, by contrast, was standing fast. She was keeping faith with what she had committed to do, and she was letting everyone know that she had hit a snag.

Watching Sara, Matt saw something in himself he never saw before. He had isolated himself. He hadn't learned to receive—to let others help him. And he hadn't learned to release, to admit in an open way that things weren't working. The result was that he'd become a little man hiding behind a curtain making reactive decisions left and right. He broke his word, changed his mind, rotated through a phalanx of consultants du jour, and exhausted his team all the while.

"Play it close to the vest" had seemed like strength in leadership to Matt. Leaders need to hold their cards after all. But Sara had just shown her cards and yet was sticking resolutely to her stated goal. It wasn't weakness in the least. She stood before him right now with the sturdiness of the mountain range that rose up to snowcaps behind her.

"It's an incredible story, Sara," Matt said, his voice low, his point understated. Sara looked at Matt and saw the passion on his face. She smiled and grimaced at the same time.

"A sob story," she admitted. "What I hope to achieve may or may not happen," she elaborated.

"That's my point, Sara," Matt continued, looking into her eyes. "You want something that's important, and it might not happen."

David fixed his gaze on to Matt the way a coach fixes his gaze on to an Olympic runner who is set in the blocks awaiting the gun. This was a moment that mattered, David knew, and what Matt would now do with it could not be predicted.

"Your dream is to race Arrow to national prominence," Matt began. He paused, not to collect his thoughts, but to lay this first stone well before rushing to the next one. Sara didn't blink.

"And your dream will take a long time to fulfill if it can be fulfilled at all," he continued. "The bigness of it—the audacity, really—is almost unbelievable." Another pause, which Sara filled with another deep breath. She hoped this was going somewhere.

"Big dreams inspire people, Sara," Matt added. Sara grimaced again, unable to suppress the thought that dreams can be too big—that she was, indeed, on a fool's errand.

"But it's much more than that, Sara." The grimace on her face was instantly gone. There was more. "You want to get horses adopted. You feel for these horses that are suffering so terribly, and you want to help them find homes. And all the while," Matt continued, now struggling to get the words past the feelings that had welled up within him, "*you're* the one who's suffered so terribly. Sara," he exclaimed, "it's *you* who needs a home!" Sara was blinking back tears.

"I have never"—Matt's voice was emphatic, the passion in his words at full force—"*ever* heard such a story! And every kid on your team is right there with you. Every kid here needs a home, Sara," he concluded, "and you're all pouring your love and hopes and tears into finding homes for these horses."

Tyler could not have been pressed harder into Matt's side, his head down, his tear-streaked face turned inward, dampening his big friend's shirt. Sara was looking at Matt with a faraway and lost look. It was sounding as though Matt had something to tell her, but she couldn't decipher the message.

"So, you're saying . . . ?" Sara didn't know how to finish the sentence.

"That this is the best story I've ever heard!" Matt answered, the gush of the words sounding like something between a laugh and a wail.

"I tell stories, Sara," Matt then exclaimed, realizing that his point had been missed entirely. "It's what I do. I motivate people—I move people—by telling them a story that makes them want to do something."

"You'll tell the story!" Sara exclaimed, the light of dawning realization spreading across her face.

"About you and everybody here, and about your goal, and about Arrow and all your efforts to train him, and about mustangs . . ." Matt's voice trailed off. He looked down at Tyler, red-faced and tucked under his arm. "And about how there are incredible kids here—and everywhere—whom people would be lucky to have as sons and daughters.

"I'll tell the story, Sara," he concluded, his face bright, "and we can start immediately!"

———◆———

Friday afternoon was a blur of activity. The excitement of Sara's charge meeting carried through lunch, and a buzz was building around the ranch as the rest of the youths heard about what had happened. Matt was going to turn Sara's plan to race Arrow into a story. "People love a good story, one with heart and heartbreak and hope," Matt had said.

An afternoon call to his New York teammates planted the seed of an idea about following in Billy Crystal's city-slicker boot prints. David offered to host Matt's senior team for a three-day hands-on team consultation at the ranch the following month. "It's how we'll pay you for the pro bono marketing work you're gonna do," he explained.

After dinner, Matt called Alice, and they talked for a long time. They wondered out loud to each other how they'd let so much build up—they'd been so close, best friends, coadventurers when they were first married. He asked Alice a question, and she didn't reject it out of hand. Indeed, while she said to him that she needed to think about it, Matt finished the conversation with a sense that she was maybe open to his proposal.

After hanging up the phone, Matt made a beeline to tell David everything. However, he was disappointed at how few words he received back from his mentor after such a momentous couple of hours of work and decisions. David listened and, when Matt was done, simply asked him to join him for an early twilight walk.

"My ex and I had a son," David said after they'd walked a few hundred yards back up into the same foothills where they'd been the night before. The field in this direction was filled with tall grass and scruffy pines scattered about, its slope gentle, the thicker grove of trees where they'd gathered around a fire the night before lying just ahead. Matt saw glimpses of a new fire sparking flashes of light through the trees and glanced over his shoulder to notice adults and youths beginning to trickle out of the dining hall and living quarters, moving in their direction.

"I never knew anything about your family," Matt replied, turning back to give David his undivided attention.

"My marriage was over long before I met you, already ruined well before I had the chance to impress you with the great success I'd become." David spoke in a clear voice. This wasn't a late-night confessional, and David wasn't spilling a pent-up sorrow in search for pity.

"You asked me how we turned a ranch for horses into a ranch for kids," David continued, "and I told you that some stuff happened."

"You said that some stuff happened, and then some other stuff happened," Matt responded, quoting the cryptic reference from the morning before.

"The stuff that happened, Matt, is that my son, John—we called him Johnny—came to see me here. Johnny was thirty, but he weighed a hundred pounds. He was six feet tall." David stopped to face his friend. "He needed money, had been using drugs since he was fourteen years old, and hoped I'd give him a hand. Reasonable of him," David added, looking down at his boots. "A son should expect his father to do something for him, and he figured he was due, which he was."

David looked back up at Matt, his gaze level. "While he was at home with his mother, he'd kept his drug use hidden. There was plenty of money—my penance, Matt. It turns out I supplied my kid with the money he used for drugs. I wanted to make up for not being there. I was killing him and my wife never knew it was going on or chose not to see it. His life fell apart after he cut his mother and me off right after high school. For over ten years I didn't know where my son was.

"C'mon," David said, hooking Matt's elbow and steering him off the pathway onto a smaller trail that led to the left of the fire circle. Just ahead appeared a small group of headstones. Matt's heart was in his throat, and then he saw the stone he knew was their destination, its engraving simple: "John David Butler—Son."

"Johnny and I spoke for about an hour the night he arrived— he was messed up, and it wasn't much of a conversation. I insisted he get some sleep, and then I lay awake the whole night. I dedicated myself that night to become the father I hadn't been. I felt I'd been given a chance to set things right, and I thought about whom I could call the next morning to help me learn how to help my son.

"But there was no next day. Johnny died in his sleep that night." A tight-lipped smile clamped back the emotions David was feeling. "I told you that we all do things we can't forgive, Matt," David continued. "We stumble, sometimes beyond all measure. There are times when our mistakes can't be fixed. Not by us," he added.

"Does John Butler have anything to do with this?" Matt asked.

"Yes and no. And your question is why I brought you up here. Yes, John is now also my son—I didn't tell you that I adopted John when he was nineteen. Turns out there's no coincidence in our shared name after all."

Matt's eyes widened at this revelation.

"And my desire to learn how to be a father was made possible by what happened to Johnny. So, yes," David rounded in on his point, "John Butler has a lot to do with this.

"But I must also say 'no,' Matt. A person might think I'm making up for my mistake—fixing what happened, so to speak. But my love for John Butler does not make up for the fact that there's a headstone standing there, and my Johnny's buried under it." David's jaw was jutted out in a resolute show of determination to say what he'd brought Matt up here to say. "John does not replace Johnny, and loving John does not make up for failing Johnny.

"Tyler needs someone to love him," he said, coming around to his point. Matt's eyes jumped up to meet his mentor's. "If the someone he needs is you, I couldn't be happier," David added, "but Tyler's not the boy you lost, and loving him—which I highly recommend—won't fix what you did."

"You said what I did could be fixed" was all Matt could say in weak retort. In the last moments, his heart had gone hard; his warm thoughts about what Tyler could do for him and Alice had turned cold. He could not remember a time when his mentor had been as hurtful as he was being right now.

Before Matt even saw it coming, David had him in an embrace, his arms tight around his young friend's neck and shoulders. "It can be fixed, Matt," David said quietly into his ear, "but *you* can't fix it. My only point here—and it matters more than anything else I could ever give you, or Tyler, for that matter— my only point is that there's no penance, no alms, no sacrifice, no works of great charity, no human effort *you* can do to fix what happened. I *didn't* say that *nobody* can fix it. And on that point," David continued, releasing his embrace but keeping one arm around his confused friend, "we've one more stop before this consultation's over."

David guided Matt down to the fire circle. The blaze was nearly six feet tall, and a chill had quickly fallen, making the fire's warmth most welcome. Everyone was assembled. David left Matt standing alone by the fire and stepped to the top of the circle.

"If I had unlimited fuel," David began without preamble, "and a jet aircraft, and I set my navigation either for due north or due south, how long would I fly?" he asked the assembly.

"Couple of hours," Bobby said. "Till you got to one of the poles."

"A short while," David answered simply. "The trip would only be as long as it takes to get to the north or the south pole.

"A verse from the book of Psalms," David then called out, his voice big and rough. "For as far as the east is from the west," he read, pausing for this new set of vectors to lock into his listeners' imaginations, "so far has God removed our transgressions from us."

David paused again, the roar of the fire quickly replacing the sound of his voice.

"We've all done things we can't forgive, friends," David then added, tonight choosing to say a few words into the vastness of the universe that pressed in on this small band. "And getting away from the things we do is not in our power." David made his remarks looking directly at Matt. "So, how far apart are east and west?" David asked, letting the question sink in. No one answered him.

"A human being can't get from east to west," David declared. "The distance is too great. The distance, in fact, is infinite, and you can't cover that distance on your own.

"Let go of what you did!" David nearly barked, still looking at Matt. "Let it go! As we say in AA, 'Let go and let God.' What we can't handle, he can."

David stopped talking, and the immensity of the scene reexerted itself, overshadowing his brief words, but powerfully underscoring them. Never in his life had Matt felt so desperate, perched so precariously on the cliff edge of himself. Unable to stand still any longer, he quickly moved away from the fire to be by himself.

David watched his friend retreat and waited to be sure that he wasn't followed by any of the youths. A few minutes, he told himself, holding back from immediately rushing after Matt. He needs a few minutes alone—important, terrible, lonely minutes. And then David would go after him. When his friend had had enough time to face his despair, David would go and offer the guidance he knew Matt needed. The work of letting go—of releasing the things he was trying to carry—would need a guide. Matt wouldn't know how to make this journey by himself.

LEADING
THE
CHEER

The midmorning drive to the airport on Saturday was less than a sixty-mile trip, and on almost any road system in the United States it should have taken an hour at most. But when combined with his trancelike state, the serpentine roadway that led back down the mountain turned Matt's sober trek into a two-and-a-quarter-hour journey. The sun was intermittently in his eyes as it rose ever higher into the morning sky or was flashing brilliantly against the steep rugged mountains to his left or right as he traced his way down from High Summit's nine thousand feet above sea level to Colorado Springs's mere six thousand. Driving through the town of Divide, Matt shook his head in bemusement. Divide, indeed. He was at a divide, and what his personal one was about was greater than a continent.

Finally through the last twisting turns in and around the Garden of the Gods, the airport now only another twenty minutes away, Matt felt his anxiety growing. It had all seemed so clear, finally, the night before. David and he had talked till after midnight, and then he'd made his choices. The course was set, and he had been prepared, as he went to bed, to live with the consequences.

Now he wasn't sure. High Summit Ranch to his back, the airport fast approaching, he felt a growing insecurity about what he had resolved to do. It could have all been so clean, he told himself as he parked his rental car. A consultation finished, notes collated and neatly packed, new plans drawn, and a couple hours of sublime first-class flight—plus drinks—would have pushed the ranch, the kids, and everything else into a softer and rapidly diminishing focus. Walking toward security, Matt shook his head, unable to suppress the grin that was spreading across his face.

I could have escaped was what he was thinking—could have, but hadn't. Standing before security, waiting patiently, he felt the wonder of being empty-handed. He'd let it all go. Just let it go. And as though to underscore the point, he'd left his luggage, clothes, and even neatly collated notes behind, all of them still tucked into the desk and dresser drawers in his room back at the ranch.

When he'd awakened in the early predawn light, he checked his voice mail. The message that greeted him held great promise, and with that promise, he'd quietly dressed and slipped out of the ranch to face his prospects.

His trip back down the mountain to this airport was so different than he'd planned, so empty-handed, so light. The only things in his pants pockets were his driver's license, a little cash, and the keys to the car that he should have returned to the rental agency hours before.

And then, like a miracle, she was there, and she was embracing and kissing him, and it was all so totally unexpected—foolish on so many levels—yet wonderful. He had asked her without notice only twelve hours before, and she'd actually come!

"I do love you, Matt" was all Alice finally said, pulling herself into him tightly. As he held her, he wondered about the big, wide, empty first-class seat that was by now at least beyond the Mississippi River, taking the phantom Matt, from whom he'd divided himself, back to New York. And he wondered about the small narrow bed back at the ranch that tonight would *not* be empty. *What an upgrade I got,* he thought, kissing his wife on the top of her jet-black mop of closely cropped hair.

"They're teaching these children how to achieve their life's biggest goals," Matt was explaining to Alice as they sat together in the outside patio of the Balanced Rock Café, buffalo burgers half eaten, the buzz of the Garden of the Gods Trading Post providing them with perfect anonymity and privacy. They needed time together before arriving into the crush of youth and curiosity back at the ranch. "Step by step, they show these youths what to do with their dreams, how to pursue them, and how to work them out. It's amazing."

"Would they show us?" Alice asked, her face a study in pain and longing. "Anybody would say that we're really successful, Matt," she implored, "but it's a joke! What about all the things we dreamed? What about our goals?"

"They'll show us," Matt answered simply but emphatically. A goal achievement team could just as well be a married couple as a corporate division, he'd figured out, or a group of golf buddies, neighbors, colleagues, or girlfriends. "What helps these kids will help my team at Lumina," he elaborated, "but it'll just as well help you and me and us together." He reached across the table to grasp Alice's hands. "Have you thought about it?" he then ventured to ask.

"It's huge, Matt." Alice paused, a look of worry in her eyes. "Of course I've thought about it. I could hardly sleep. But, honestly, I can't even begin to imagine it."

Matt nodded his understanding. Tyler shouldn't be imagined, he was thinking—couldn't be, for that matter. Tyler needed to be experienced firsthand. He just squeezed Alice's hand.

"Looks like we're sharing a single bed tonight," he added. Matt wanted to give his wife time, a little breathing room, some lightheartedness.

She raised her eyebrows and peered at her husband over the reading glasses she also wore to eat. "That used to work quite nicely, as I seem to distantly recall," she replied playfully.

"How did we end up so far apart?" Alice suddenly went on, her voice immediately stripped of its playfulness and now filled with grief.

"The king-sized bed did it," Matt deadpanned. "It's so big I need a map."

"The king-sized bed and every other bloody thing we've stuffed into our lives," Alice agreed, her voice edged with anger. "Work and stress and hurt and so much silence." Her words were spoken across the table with complete directness and no recrimination. She held Matt's gaze with a look of tremendous sorrow. "So we filled up our lives with more and more stuff and ended up both pushed out onto the street to live like beggars. Is any of this what you actually wanted?" Alice added, her voice a plea. "I wanted adventure and togetherness. And all we got is busy and burned."

"I watch these kids, Alice," Matt replied, "and the process for goal achievement they're taught gets them the adventure that they want and the togetherness. They learn how to pursue their goals and achieve them, but what's really going on is that they're being shown the purpose of their lives. And they get to have their adventure in the company of friends. Life is crazy," Matt went on, his voice now very animated. "All these abandoned kids already know what we don't know. They're learning what we need to learn, how to follow your dreams and achieve your goals. And even more importantly, how to get your life turned back on, to work with others, and to help each other.

"What I should say," Matt added more reflectively, "is that life is wonderful." He looked at Alice—really looked—and felt grateful. "We could complain that we're only getting a chance to learn what we need to learn in our forties—that it's too late, I mean. But it isn't too late. And I think most people never ever learn it at all."

———◆———

"Matt and I spoke last evening, Alice, about how important it is to know that an adopted child can't replace some other child, one you lost or one you dreamed of having." David and John were sitting with Matt and Alice in David's office. David had asked Matt and Alice to spend some time with him when they returned before meeting the youths on the ranch. He had also asked Matt if it would be okay for John to join them.

The warmth with which David greeted Alice when they'd finally arrived back after their long lunch meant a great deal to Matt. David had walked quickly toward them before they'd finished getting Alice's luggage from the car and had embraced her with a father's ardor. Alice could not have been more powerfully swept into this new circle.

"Matt told me," Alice said simply, reaching a hand over to grasp her husband's. He'd told her many things at lunch, all of them good things, she felt, yet things she needed time to process.

David nodded his head, encouraged by everything he was seeing, and made his decision to proceed.

"It goes the other way around, too," he added, a look of puzzlement appearing on both Matt's and Alice's faces. "A new mom and dad don't replace the mom and dad a child loses," David clarified. "These kids desperately need new moms and dads, but the operational word is 'new.' They'll always still have lost the old ones."

"For the ones who knew their parents," Matt offered. He meant that David's comment might not apply to every adopted child, maybe not to the ones adopted at birth.

"Every situation's different, Matt," John chimed in. "Every child's different. So you're right to suggest that things can't be generalized. We're talking about little human beings here, every one unique."

"But there are still patterns," David continued, "and even kids adopted as infants face questions other kids don't. Where'd my dad go? Why'd my mom give me up? Didn't they want me? Is something wrong with me?"

"Am I lovable?" John added, cutting to the heart of the matter. "People who really understand the grief felt by adopted kids sometimes call this the 'primal wound.' It's a deep, intimate trauma that you need to understand, Matt and Alice, before you go too far forward in your thoughts about Tyler."

Matt and Alice looked at each other, their thoughts sober. "You're warning us," Alice said, directing her comment to John, "that an adopted child feels more than gratitude toward his new parents." She knew that this was true, of course; she wasn't naïve. It made sense to her to actually state it. "There are struggles," she added.

John's smile couldn't have been warmer. He really liked Alice—a sentiment David shared—and let it show. "I've brought David nothing but struggle, that's for sure," he said playfully, "but the papers were signed seven years ago, so he's stuck with me."

"I needed John in my life as much as he needed me," David said quietly, looking over at his son, "more, truth be told."

"Oh, that's a lot of bull!" John laughed, his face radiant. "This is a fight I'm never going to let him win," he added.

"What does it look like?" Alice pressed on. "The struggle, I mean."

"In broad brushstrokes, Alice," David answered, "you get one of two kinds of behavior to look for. One, the child does things you don't approve of to test if you'll reject him. Is your love for real, or is it just a hobby? A kid can work hard to get himself rejected by his new parents. And he hopes against all hope that his efforts will fail, though he'll never let you in on any of this. In all likelihood, he won't understand it himself. He'll just flail and rage and test and sabotage."

David gave them a moment to absorb what he'd just told them.

"Quite a rude disappointment to an adoptive parent who's trying to make up for an earlier wrong," Matt said.

"A huge disappointment," David agreed, "unless you realize where this child's coming from. Unless you know that it's not about you is what I mean."

David and Matt locked eyes for a moment. As enraged as he'd been at his mentor the night before, Matt was now utterly grateful for what he'd learned, what David had helped him understand and do.

"What's the other kind?" Alice asked, persistent in her questions.

"The perfect child," John answered, his face uncharacteristically devoid of its customary smile. "My kind," he then added, there being no joke intended. "You spend years trying to earn a mom and dad, and finally you get one, so you have to be just perfect 'cause you know that one screwup and you're gone!" John then smiled again, a sad smile, and looked over in the direction of David.

"The old man needed to teach me that perfect was impossible. That being loved had nothing to do with being perfect. That it's always a gift, never a right or a reward. I thought that the kids who had parents had a right to be loved and that the rest of us had to earn it. David taught me that it's the same for both kinds of kid; love is a gift. Always! Once that sank in, I started to know what it felt like to breathe."

———

"You can't imagine how important our parties are, Matt," David started to explain. John had departed to attend to his duties, and Alice had gone to the kitchen to help set up for the planned Saturday evening festivities. She did this in part because the kitchen was always where she wanted to be when a party was in the works. More to the point, Tyler was on kitchen crew. It had been agreed that a chance to meet Tyler apart from Matt—no strange dynamics of expectation—was a good idea. Tyler knew nothing of Matt's thoughts, wouldn't know who Alice was, and wouldn't be in performance mode. Alice had agreed to come to the ranch and check things out. She had not agreed to step into an emotional trap and insisted on keeping control of the steps she might take. David had agreed with this plan and would have laid it out the same way himself.

"Everything you've seen so far with our Engagement Equation is effective in getting the kids moving in the right direction," David continued, "but aiming in the right direction is one thing. Staying on course and remaining motivated to give your very best effort over time is another thing. So let me cheat on my rules again, Matt, and fill out the rest of the picture for you. I was going to introduce you to the third capability in our equation on your next visit," he added and gave Matt a broad grin as he got up from his seat to write on the large sheet of paper hanging on the wall amid the dozens of horse and youth photos to the right of his big desk.

"By way of review, trust is the baseline character requirement of leadership." David wrote as he talked. "We work every day to close the say-do gap by keeping our promises to our staff and kids. It's the foundational work we do to set a stage of trust with our workers."

"It's a multiplier," Matt interjected. "You write T times the Cs, rather than T plus the Cs," he added.

David smiled. "An astute observation, Matt. Trust is not an additive. If trust is zero, your results will be zero, regardless of how strong your capabilities are.

"So, you've been introduced to the first capability," he continued. "Challenge is the preparation stage. With clear vision in mind, the leader lays out the plans, fitting strengths to roles. Do you remember what I stressed here?"

"Learning to receive," Matt answered. "Your team brings you value, and you must look for it and learn to appreciate what's there, instead of focusing on what's not there."

David wrote the word "Challenge," adding the words "preparation stage—plans, strengths, roles," as well as "learn to receive" just beneath.

"And the second capability?"

"Charge. Both you and Teddy stressed that in this stage, you should expect your plans to go off track. So you innovate, scan, adjust," he added, showing his mentor he was ready for more.

"Charge," David wrote, adding "implementation stage—innovate, scan, adjust" and "learn to release" underneath.

"What's the importance of learning to release, Matt?"

"Course corrections are normal. You have to let go of what's not working."

"And as we discussed, your mistakes too. You have to let go of the little mistakes and the big ones. Move on."

David and Matt smiled at each other. They'd covered a lot of territory in a very short time.

"And the third capability?" Matt's smile had broadened. "Let me guess it has something to do with throwing a party." David simply filled out the chart, writing the words "evaluation stage—measure, reward, (re)prepare."

David then added the words "learn to rejoice" to the chart, completing his review and update.

"The evaluation stage, when carefully designed to reinforce your purpose and your plans, produces kids who finally start to act like owners rather than unwilling laborers. The party, as you call it, locks the entire process into place."

"Can you tell me more about this?" Matt asked, now sitting up very straight, his eyes fixed on David's words on the newsprint.

"The first thing a goal achievement leader does is make sure that the goal and the plan are crystal clear. Leaders do this with their teams in the challenge stage. When team members show they can clearly and accurately present the leader's goals and objectives, we give it a cheer.

"The second thing we do is a constant review of progress against our goals. The implementation stage provides lots of celebration points, Matt. Every positive step gets celebrated, every adjustment gets celebrated, and every abandonment of effort that isn't working gets celebrated. We throw That Didn't

$$T \times 3C = E$$
Engagement Equation

T (closing "the say-do gap")

Trust (the leader's credibility)

$3C$ (closing "the paycheck-purpose gap")

Challenge (preparation stage)

Plans, strengths, roles

Learn to <u>receive</u>

Charge (implementation stage)

Innovate, scan, adjust

Learn to <u>release</u>

Cheer (evaluation stage)

Measure, reward, (re)prepare

Learn to <u>rejoice</u>

Work! parties," David added, "right alongside We Did It! parties. If it helps us make progress, we cheer it.

"I told you that we teach these kids how to lead in such a way that the switch gets flipped from off to on. Way back on Wednesday, if you can recall back that far," he added, smiling warmly.

Matt nodded his head. David had laid out the Engagement Equation for him, but he still hadn't explained how all of this flips the switch to full engagement.

"What I didn't tell you is that the research also diagnoses the cause of worker disengagement."

Matt's gaze was now level, his eyes unblinking.

"It's a lack of trust in leadership, Matt, not just personal trust in the leader's integrity, but systemic trust in the whole operational discipline of the organization. At one level, workers don't trust that leaders will do what they say."

"The say-do gap," Matt responded.

"At a deeper level, workers don't trust that the challenge they were given will be remembered down the line when stuff goes wrong. A little setback and to hell with the purpose and the goal. Workers watch their leaders cover their behinds all the time or throw their plans to the wind at the slightest provocation. You know it's true, Matt.

"Or the project succeeds," David continued, more animated now than ever. "The goal was reached and it's evaluation time, bonus time, promotion time. How many examples can you give me," David asked, his bearing electric, "of when a boss tells a worker to accomplish something in a certain way and for one reason or another the worker who did his part is overlooked or, worse, punished for doing exactly what he or she was asked to do?

"Why on earth bring your whole self to the job under these circumstances, right?" David was imploring Matt to understand the point. "If your boss is fickle and undisciplined, sets out an important challenge and then abandons it at the first sign of difficulty, or more routinely, doesn't carefully tie the evaluations and rewards to what he said he wanted . . ." David left the sentence unfinished.

"Better to play it safe and see how things turn out," Matt filled in, feeling very ashamed. He'd blamed Randy for losing his drive and for becoming uncommitted. Randy had turned into the perfect example of a disengaged worker, and in his mind, Matt had blamed him for lots of things as he'd sat alone in his office staring at one pathetic report after another.

And the thought of Molly only deepened his remorse. Where Randy had become apathetic and noncommittal, Molly had become hard and bitter. She was worse than disengaged; Matt had already begun to contemplate ways to get rid of her for her growing negativity. And it was he, Matt, who had hurt her, he now realized. He'd robbed her of the reward for work well done, penalized her with what he'd thought of as a promotion, and blamed her for everything that had resulted from his own poor leadership.

Talk about fickle and undisciplined. Talk about not tying rewards to the positive things that were accomplished. It sickened Matt to think about what he'd done; it was unwitting on his part, to be sure, but he'd done it nonetheless.

Deb was another matter, and Matt resolved to ask her how she kept herself so positive. She remained engaged, but it was no credit to him. It was as if she showed up for work already fulfilled rather than coming to work in order to get fulfilled. He was very fortunate, he realized, to have her.

"All of it's trust, Matt," David added, "trust in you and trust in your operational discipline."

Matt nodded soberly. He was getting it.

"Turns out," David continued, "that, aside from a couple of scoundrels, most workers would actually like to like their jobs. Most workers actually have ideas about making improvements at work that they'd like to share. Most workers would like to go home at the end of the day and tell someone a story about how they made a difference. But why bother."

"If your boss can't be counted on to stay the course," Matt filled in.

"If your operational practices lack the daily discipline and the tools required to stick to the purposes and plans of the enterprise," David elaborated.

A silence fell between them.

"So the *T* is the leader's necessary character baseline. The leader must close the say-do gap."

It was well-rehearsed territory and required no response from Matt.

"The *C*s are the imperatives of daily operational discipline and consistency. The leader must close the paycheck-purpose gap."

"Sara mentioned that. What does it mean?"

"Great leaders take tremendous care to tie their inspiring speeches to the daily, picayunish operational realities. What's stated in the great purpose shows up again when it's party time. It's not just words is what it means, Matt!

"I can't explain it, but your credibility as a leader hasn't been fully established until there's a party. When you stick to your word all the way through to the party, your followers finally know that you really said what you said, meant what you meant, and want what you want." David walked back up to the newsprint and wrote his formula on the top of the newsprint:

$$T \times 3C = E$$

"Work the equation," David concluded, "and your business becomes more than a paycheck to your employees. It becomes part of their sense of purpose and meaning. Work the equation, and the result is true engagement. And, Matt," David added with emphasis, "when your team is truly engaged, hang on to your hat!"

"That's the warning you gave me on the phone, David," Matt interjected, chuckling.

David looked puzzled.

"I asked you what hands-on meant, and you said that hands are real good for hanging on to my hat. Scared me half to death, I must tell you."

David remembered and laughed along with his younger charge, enjoying the realization of how far Matt had come in this short while.

"I told you hands are good for more than that," David retorted.

"Wasn't a fair contest, David."

"No. Not fair. But you have to know that I never saw this bond you have with Tyler coming. I was sure that, if there was any blood in your veins, you'd be touched. But Tyler is the architect of everything else. He chose you."

"And I him," Matt responded, his voice quiet, his face reflective.

"Nervous?"

"No. I'm at peace. What should be will be. Alice and Tyler will connect, or they won't. She comes first. Tyler has no future with me if he has no future with Alice."

David's eyes filled with gratitude. He could not imagine hearing better words than these. Matt and Alice were going to be okay. This was foundational, and nothing he hoped for Tyler came before it.

"So, let's head over. Time to party!" David said these words with a sense of profound consequence. They were about to learn something important, and until they walked outside and crossed the courtyard to the dining hall, they'd have no idea what the future was about to become.

——◄•►——

Matt preceded David through the doorway to the dining hall, crossed the threshold, and froze in his tracks. The scene was bedlam. Kids were stringing ribbon across great sections of the ceiling; others were working over a helium tank, blowing up balloons; others were setting plates, cups, and silverware around tables; and still others were hanging a giant banner in the front of the room bearing the words "Matt James: Official Cowboy!" He'd thought this was Sara's sixteenth birthday party. Even though her actual birth date wasn't until tomorrow, he'd bought the ruse. They were going to throw Sara a big party, and wasn't it great that Matt was staying an extra day to join in? He was stunned by the beehive of energized happiness abuzz in the room, all of it marshaled for his sake.

But this scene of good-spirited chaos was not what had stopped him in his tracks. Across the room, facing him from the far side of a worktable, stood Alice and Tyler, oblivious to his arrival and immersed in the task of icing a great sheet of birthday cake. They both had icing on their faces—clearly the work of mutual tomfoolery—as well as on their hands. They both were laughing, pointing at their masterpiece, and exchanging ideas for its improvement. And they were both leaning in toward each other in an easy closeness, Alice with one hand resting on Tyler's shoulder, and Tyler tucked in close beside her, his eyes glancing up again and again to catch hers, to catch her nods of approval, to catch her smiles and acknowledgments.

And they looked alike. Jet-black mops of closely cut, tou-sled hair, pale white skin, dark penetrating eyes, faces that often wore a look of uncertainty. He hadn't thought of it before this moment. Tyler tugged at his heart in some of the same ways Alice did—the longing, the guardedness, and the hidden ca-pacity for joy that could break free from its restraints and fill his entire being with light.

Alice looked up, saw Matt across the room, and leaned down to say something to Tyler. She kept her eyes on her hus-band as she spoke quietly into his ear. Tyler looked up, spotted Matt across the room, and nodded his head in answer to what-ever she had just said to him. Tyler then said something else to Alice, both of them now watching him, Alice now taking her turn nodding. And then Alice smiled across the room, her eyes penetrating the distance to capture her husband's attention. She leaned down to Tyler a second time and said something else to him, her lips close to his ear. Tyler cocked his head, the lines of his forehead furrowed as he tried to put together the pieces of information he was being given. She said one more thing, his eyes flared in astonishment, and then he grinned his biggest smile yet, gesturing wildly for Matt to come over to where they were standing. This arrangement proving to be unsatisfactorily slow, Tyler bolted from his position beside Alice to meet Matt halfway across the room in order to escort him back to his right-ful place beside the woman he had just learned was not only his newest friend, but his other newest friend's wife.

Matt gave Tyler a hug, took his hand, and strolled across the room toward the lady in waiting. He gave her a hug, too, and then a kiss on the lips. Tyler watched in embarrassment and awe.

Noticing the cake finally, Matt let out a huge guffaw. Crudely, but not without artfulness, Alice and Tyler had iced a picture of a running horse, legs stretched out in full flight, with the figure of a man—no doubts as to which man—clutching with all his might to the pommel with one hand and to his hat with the other. Across the top of the cake, they had written in icing, "Matthew James—Ride 'em, Cowboy."

"She's your wife" was the first thing Tyler said. It was a happy exclamation, but also slightly tutorial, as though he were filling Matt in on a crucial point.

Matt tousled Tyler's hair and looked at Alice. "She is indeed, Tyler. She's my wife." Alice regarded Matt with a loving gaze. A page had turned in their relationship, she was thinking, and the hopes she used to have were coming back to life.

"So how'd she treat you?" Matt continued, speaking to the boy with a tone of confidentiality, as though Alice weren't standing right in front of them, hearing their conversation loud and clear.

"I like her," Tyler beamed, his eyes trained on Alice.

"Me, too," Matt replied, standing before his wife as an art lover would stand before a favorite masterpiece.

The party was like no other Matt had ever attended. Never having been roasted or honored, he found it overwhelming to hear men and women, boys and girls speak about the value they had received through knowing him. How could this be? His fourth night on the ranch would be tonight. He'd barely gotten acquainted. And now the children were verbalizing, point by point, what Matt had offered them during this visit, what they had received and learned from him. It humiliated him to think about the fact that he led a corporate division and had done nothing remotely approaching the power of this for any of his fine people. *And a child shall lead them,* he thought, unable to locate in his memory the source for this ancient quotation.

"Matt, Saturday and Sunday nights are spent indoors, rather than out at the fire circle." David had brought the long—and sometimes hilarious—round of affirmations and observations to a close and had taken his place at the front of the ranch's assembly to wrap up the evening's celebration. Everyone was on their feet, circled into a loose knot of bodies. Alice took Matt's hand, and Tyler moved in to stand behind them. Feeling the child's warmth pressed in against them, they lifted their interlocked fingers back and over his head to draw him forward between them.

"I promised you I would teach you what you need to know to turn your division around back in New York. I didn't mention that I'd have help."

Matt gazed around the group, amazed at their evident interest in his well-being and their generosity of spirit and time.

"I have one final thing to say to you before we bid you farewell. I've been stressing the importance of getting your people fully engaged. And I told you a little while ago that it's all about trust." He waited to receive Matt's acknowledgment of this point. "And several times during your visit I've revealed to you a deep truth that leaders must grasp if they want to create a company of full engagement."

Now Matt's head stopped nodding. This "deep truth" he'd somehow missed.

"No worries, friend," David continued, his face kind. "I showed it to you, but I never straight out told you.

"'Every Child a Hope, Every Child a Home.' Our ranch's tagline," David began. "Hope springs up from belonging,

Matt," he continued, "and belonging is experienced in a circle of people who trust and rely upon each another. Each one has something to give. Each one is able to receive.

"Home is what we call that place of belonging. When we search for our home, it is belonging we are searching for. We're working our tails off here to find each of these children a home," David added, his voice rising in passion for the words he was speaking. "But first and foremost, we are creating home right here. Or to say it in more businesslike terms, we're creating a culture of full engagement here at the ranch. At High Summit, we create a culture of trustworthiness and welcome—which is what home is—in which these children discover that it's safe and good to bring their whole selves to the adventure.

"Our Engagement Equation doesn't just make the work go better, Matt," David concluded. "It creates an entirely new culture in which people choose to invest their whole selves. The deep truth is that leaders don't actually ever engage people."

Matt blinked, waiting for his mentor to connect the dots.

"People engage *themselves*," David said. "They do their part if we do ours. Leaders make the difference first—we set the stage. And then followers make their difference by bringing all of who they are to the enterprise. We must do our part—we must work the Engagement Equation with integrity and daily discipline—and then they'll do theirs."

All eyes were on Matt. David's words had created in the group a feeling of bigness and significance. His message was aimed at each of them, they all felt, but it was also aimed in a special way at Matt. Matt knew that David had just wrapped up this business consultation.

"A reading from Paul's Letter to the Romans," David said, bringing everyone back from their private reflections. "'This life you received from God has replaced your old life of slavery and fear. No longer castaways and slaves, your new life is a life of adoption, for you now belong to the home of God. Now you can live adventurously, greeting God every day with a childlike What's next, Daddy?'"

"Time for bed, everybody," David added, his eyes trained on Matt and Alice. "Sleep! Dream! Be restored! Tomorrow's a new beginning. Let's find out what it holds!"

NEW ENGAGEMENT

Seventeen hundred miles later, Matt was back in familiar urban chaos. The red-white-and-blue-lit Empire State Building and an overly talkative limo driver told him he was home. He directed the limo to take him straight to the office, even though it was 1:30 in the morning. Only Bob Herman, the night guard, was there to greet him. "Come into my office, Bob," Matt invited. "Do you have a minute to talk?"

With a puzzled but interested audience, Matt laid out a plan to create the structure of goal achievement teams throughout his division and to introduce the Engagement Equation as the process his team would use to improve their results. To the guard's bemusement, Matt also printed out photos of wild mustangs, Rocky Mountain scenes, and children to post around his office.

Bob took it in with an interested expression on his face. He was thinking that Matt had lost it—and had become friendlier. But listening to Matt beat strolling the floors.

For the first time in his career, Matt then slept on his office couch, awakening after two hours to shower in the workout locker room. As he moved around the building in the predawn, he strained his ears for the sounds of kids laughing and chatting as they started their daily routines. Instead, he heard the brief musical boot-ups of office computers and the increasingly frequent warbling of various cell-phone ring tones.

Matt walked to the water cooler outside the conference room. As he filled his cup, he took a moment to go over the events of the past few days. How could he adequately tell his team that his world was changing? Could he bring them along with him? Getting them to the ranch next month would fill in much, but he wasn't sure what to say in the meantime. Absently drinking the last of his water, he crumpled the tiny cup and threw it away, turning to face the conference room door.

His right palm closed around the metal knob of the teak door. Turning it and pushing the door open, he was greeted by the red-orange sunlight from the New York morning that was spilling in through the windows. His mind reeled backward to his first sunset in Colorado that he had shared with David. He felt like closing his eyes to picture it again but heard someone call his name from behind him.

It was Randy, his lead salesman.

"Morning, Matt. Sounds like you had an interesting trip."

"You have no idea," he smiled, putting an arm around Randy's shoulder to guide him into the room with him. Surreptitiously, Randy peeked down at his shoulder, upon which Matt's hand was making its historic first visit.

Half an hour later Room 43C had filled with Matt's team, all gathered around the long mahogany conference table. Standing up, Matt took his place at the head of the table, cleared his throat, opened his mouth to begin his remarks, and then closed it again. He'd taken in the apprehensive faces as well as the jaded ones and knew that there was a tremendous amount of ground to cover—if it could be covered at all.

"I need to start with an apology," he said, his face warm, his gaze level.

Multiple pairs of eyes that had been glaring downward or staring off into the distance suddenly focused on him. No one had ever heard the word "apology" in any of Matt's previous remarks. Was he getting ready to resign? Was he about to announce dire news?

"I've had a chance to think about a great many things this week, and I realize that I've not been a good leader for you or a good teammate. Not by a long shot."

Matt had everybody's attention now, and while not all of it was charitably inclined, all of it was at least in full agreement.

"I want to try to set things right, but I can't do that without your help. I'd like another chance if you'd be willing to give it to me." Matt paused for a moment. "I know that I don't deserve it," he said more quietly, "but I'd be so very grateful if you'd join me for another try."

"Absolutely" came a response from the other end of the table. It was Randy, the member of the team he least expected to speak first. "I'm in," Deb chimed. Molly glanced away, her eyes hard, her face disbelieving. Other teammates added their affirmations, some seeming to do so genuinely and others less convincingly. Matt saw the diverse responses and considered himself well treated by it all.

Leaning stiffly back in his chair and folding his hands together, Randy asked, "So what do you have in mind, boss?"

Matt laid out what he'd learned, and as he spoke, he gained more of the group's interest. Matt outlined on the white boards what he had learned about goal achievement teams and the Engagement Equation. He showed them the three capabilities in the equation and walked them through the Engagement Planning Workbook he had received just before departing the ranch. He described as best he could how they were going to need to start from square one, building dependability throughout the chain of work from initial project descriptions all the way to measures and rewards.

It was a new experience for him as well as for his team, but he saw energy build as he made room for discovery and give-and-take. When Matt gave specific examples from his own leadership that illustrated his mistakes and failures—how he had broken trust or had caused operational derailments that hurt and discouraged the group—he finally gained everyone's full attention. Molly's face showed that she was going to wait and see, but Matt considered this a real sign of progress.

Randy suggested they try the Engagement Equation as a pilot project—take one of their newer initiatives, chart the entire project using the workbook, and then run it with close attention to the model they were learning.

"What about doing two pilots?" Deb asked, as all heads turned her way. "You called us about Sara Jarrel," she elaborated. "Wouldn't it be natural to shape the project we do for her using these tools? She already works with them."

Matt then told his team about some of the more personal dimensions of his trip. His enthusiasm built as he spoke, and the fact that he had been so deeply touched by his experience helped his teammates in their own feelings toward him. He told them about Sara and John, about David's son Johnny, and about Tyler. He told them that Alice had decided to stay an extra two days, and that he was nervous—no, terrified—about what might happen next. Would Alice determine that the answer was no? He couldn't bear to think about it. Would she determine that the answer was yes? He hadn't a clue about how they were going to bring a nine-year-old son into their lives. And he told them about his hopes for their team visit to High Summit the next month, both to advance their own work and to help Sara's goal achievement team.

The team decided at the close of the meeting to gather the following morning to hold a miniretreat for themselves.

The next day, the retreat started dramatically. After most of the informal conversations died down, Matt again addressed his team.

"Thank you for making time to do this," he began. "I promise you that our time together today will be interesting. Randy?" he asked, a small smile playing on the edges of his face, "you want to take it away?"

"If you'll follow us outside," Randy chimed in, rising quickly to his feet and strolling out the door. Randy and Matt had stayed after work to talk—Randy's request—and ended the evening talking through what they would do the next day when the staff reconvened. Randy guided them, not to the front of the office, but to the utility entrance and docks in the rear, where they were greeted by the sight of waist-high stacks of neatly piled paper in the center of the alley.

Seeing everyone's puzzled looks, Matt spoke up. "If you take a closer look, you'll see that piled before you are our division's current strategic plans and budgets."

Several eyes widened in fear at the thought that they were going to have to go back through all of this stuff.

"Randy, you worked on much of this. Would you show us what our first assignment is?"

"Gladly," Randy replied. And with that, Randy took an armful of paper and heaved it into one of the shiny steel dumpsters parked in a row behind the building. Matt was quick on his heals with an armful of his own. "Mind giving us a hand?" Randy deadpanned to the astonished team. "This stuff's heavy."

He needed to say no more. With a glee that Matt didn't miss, his team descended upon their chore and in mere seconds

had collectively scraped up all the artifacts of their dismal performance and transferred them into the dumpster.

"Gather around, folks," Randy invited the rest of the team.
"This is a celebration. A celebration of letting go of the past
and building the future together."

With an audience of a few concerned-looking security per-
sonnel who'd wandered out of Lumina's building to discover
what was going on—and sneak in a smoke—Matt gathered his
team in a semicircle around the alleyway dumpster. More than a
few snickers and giggles erupted when several of the women
suggested they link arms, and with some embarrassment and dis-
comfort the team formed a human chain around the dumpster
as though gathered for a religious ritual around a sacred totem.

"Guys are nuts . . ." was spoken loudly enough for the
group to hear above the general din of their own guffaws and
exclamations. One of the security officers had raised his voice
louder than intended while making a much longer and, for
the most part, less polite comment to another bystander in the
gallery.

"It's a party day, friends!" Matt then declared. "And this is
our first celebration. What shall we call it?"

"Happy Toss-the-Stuff-That-Failed Day!" one person offered. "We tried it, it didn't work, we're moving on!" said another. "The old Matt is dead! Long live Matt!" said another,
this more daring suggestion igniting a burst of laughter from
the group with Matt joining in happily.

As the team dispersed from their little hand-holding ritual,
milling about and chatting with each other like it was a cock-
tail party, Matt surveyed the group with brand new eyes. It was
what they would do together that mattered—what they would
learn together. He brought vision and imagination to his team;
he knew this was why he'd been tapped to step up to a new level

of leadership several years earlier. But in this circle, he now saw, were the strengths to translate possibility into reality. And if he appreciated what was standing right here in this circle, had the courage to let go of his own need to control things, and made room for everyone to own the process, anything was possible. Good things were possible.

Matt remembered the vision he'd had of his mentor staring up at him from his reflection in the conference table only two weeks ago. *It's not the end, Matt,* he had heard David say, humor and hopefulness in the voice. *It's a beginning.*

Matt remembered the dream that had awakened him during his first night on the ranch. He thought he'd heard the cry of a son who was lost. And with his second disturbing night, he'd discovered that it was partly his own voice that he had heard. It was he who felt alone and lost, lost to his own hopes, his sense of purpose, the things he most loved.

It's both strange and wonderful, Matt thought. He was now firmly in the presence of total uncertainty. He didn't know how this was going to turn out, what his team would be able to do under his leadership, what Alice was thinking today as she flew home to be with him, or what tomorrow would hold. Matt smiled as he considered how open and unknown his future had become, and he smiled as he watched the pleasure and good spirit of his teammates chatting happily like buddies gathered after work at the pub. He smiled at the realization that he wasn't alone anymore and—all uncertainties aside—he wasn't lost.

<hr />

Matt James caught a glare from the security officer as he moved too fast—was actually running, truth be told—toward

Alice as she cleared the security line at LaGuardia. He had her in his arms in a gigantic embrace, and she had him in hers.

"I'm so glad to have you back, Alice," Matt said, speaking the words softly, his mouth close to her ear. He knew that the course of his future was about to be revealed, felt the enormity of this moment, and was at peace. He had Alice. The future was, for this moment, unknown. And all was well.

Alice answered Matt with a tighter squeeze and then pulled back enough to look up into her husband's eyes. She saw tears in Matt's eyes and a great warmth on his face. There were tears in her own eyes, too. She felt all the sadness and grief of their years of drift and was glad for the beginning of renewal in their closeness and love. She smiled at her husband, blinking her eyes to clear her sight of him, to clear her sight for him, to show him what her eyes held.

"I've got news, Matt," Alice said.

$T \times 3C = E$
Engagement Equation

T (closing "the say-do gap")

Trust (the leader's credibility)

$3C$ (closing "the paycheck-purpose gap")

Challenge (preparation stage—clarity)
  Raw potential: plans, strengths, roles
  The learning: to <u>receive</u> the gifts at hand

Charge (implementation stage—constancy)
  Routine process: innovate, scan, adjust
  The learning: to <u>release</u> what isn't working

Cheer (evaluation stage—celebration)
  Real product: measure, reward, (re)prepare
  The learning: to <u>rejoice</u> in every gain, large
  or small

E (closing "the work-live gap")

Engagement (the organization's culture)

Taking the Next Step

For free-to-use Goal Achievement Work Tools, or to buy a Goal Achievement Leaders Journal based on the principles and ideas contained in this book, please visit

www.tenthousandhorses.com

Sara's Goal Achievement Journal, as well as planning tools and exercises utilizing the Engagement Equation, $T \times 3C = E$, will allow you to translate your purpose and goals into clear team plans as well as implementation and evaluation systems.

For additional resources on children, horses, and adoption, visit

www.tenthousandhorses.com/adoption

ABOUT THE AUTHORS

▲

JOHN STAHL-WERT, DMin, works with organizations that want to build great leaders who bring out the very best in their people. John provides keynote programs to executives and managers around the world on servant leadership, workforce performance, and leadership growth. A working CEO, John heads the Pittsburgh Leadership Foundation where he and his staff employ entrepreneurial and business-minded approaches to social change that have been replicated in over fifty cities around the United States. Along with Ken Jennings, John is coauthor of the international best seller *The Serving Leader*, published in eight languages. Contact him at john@johnstahlwert.com.

KEN JENNINGS, PhD, focuses on helping leaders become better coaches and lead with purpose. Through Third River Partners, he consults on the development of teams while achieving breakthroughs in critical projects. A graduate of the United States Air Force Academy and Purdue University, Ken works with the top management of leading global companies to implement innovative approaches to organizational effectiveness and leadership development. He is coauthor of *Changing Health Care* and along with John Stahl-Wert is the co-author of the international best seller *The Serving Leader*, published in eight languages. Contact him at ken@3rd-river.com.

About Berrett-Koehler Publishers

Berrett-Koehler is an independent publisher dedicated to an ambitious mission: Creating a World That Works for All.

We believe that to truly create a better world, action is needed at all levels—individual, organizational, and societal. At the individual level, our publications help people align their lives with their values and with their aspirations for a better world. At the organizational level, our publications promote progressive leadership and management practices, socially responsible approaches to business, and humane and effective organizations. At the societal level, our publications advance social and economic justice, shared prosperity, sustainability, and new solutions to national and global issues.

A major theme of our publications is "Opening Up New Space." They challenge conventional thinking, introduce new ideas, and foster positive change. Their common quest is changing the underlying beliefs, mindsets, institutions, and structures that keep generating the same cycles of problems, no matter who our leaders are or what improvement programs we adopt.

We strive to practice what we preach—to operate our publishing company in line with the ideas in our books. At the core of our approach is *stewardship*, which we define as a deep sense of responsibility to administer the company for the benefit of all of our "stakeholder" groups: authors, customers, employees, investors, service providers, and the communities and environment around us.

We are grateful to the thousands of readers, authors, and other friends of the company who consider themselves to be part of the "BK Community." We hope that you, too, will join us in our mission.

Be Connected

Visit Our Website

Go to www.bkconnection.com to read exclusive previews and excerpts of new books, find detailed information on all Berrett-Koehler titles and authors, browse subject-area libraries of books, and get special discounts.

Subscribe to Our Free E-Newsletter

Be the first to hear about new publications, special discount offers, exclusive articles, news about bestsellers, and more! Get on the list for our free e-newsletter by going to www.bkconnection.com.

Get Quantity Discounts

Berrett-Koehler books are available at quantity discounts for orders of ten or more copies. Please call us toll-free at (800) 929-2929 or email us at bkp.orders@aidcvt.com.

Host a Reading Group

For tips on how to form and carry on a book reading group in your workplace or community, see our website at www.bkconnection.com.

Join the BK Community

Thousands of readers of our books have become part of the "BK Community" by participating in events featuring our authors, reviewing draft manuscripts of forthcoming books, spreading the word about their favorite books, and supporting our publishing program in other ways. If you would like to join the BK Community, please contact us at bkcommunity@bkpub.com.